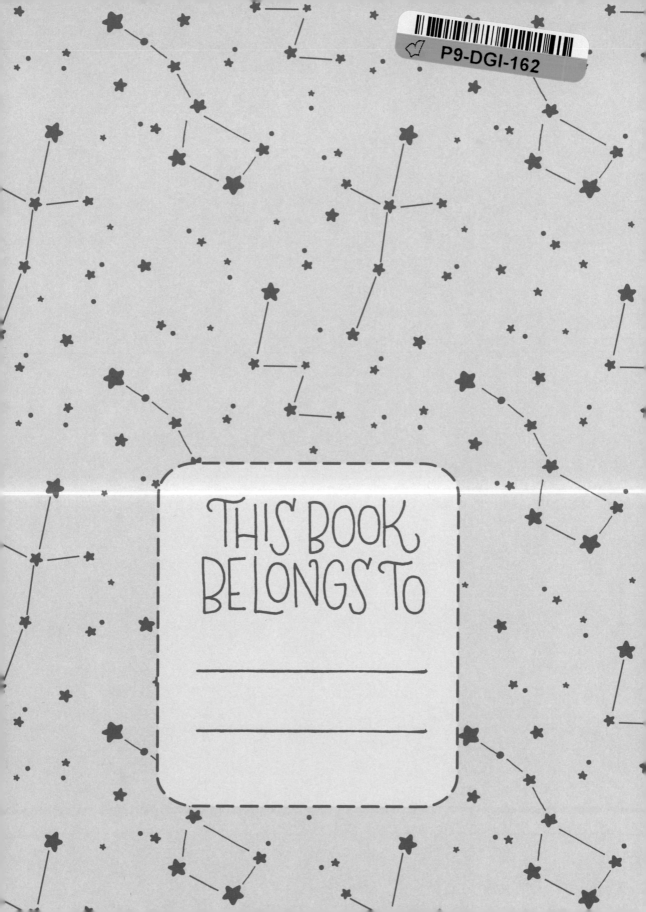

THIS BOOK
BELONGS TO

_____

_____

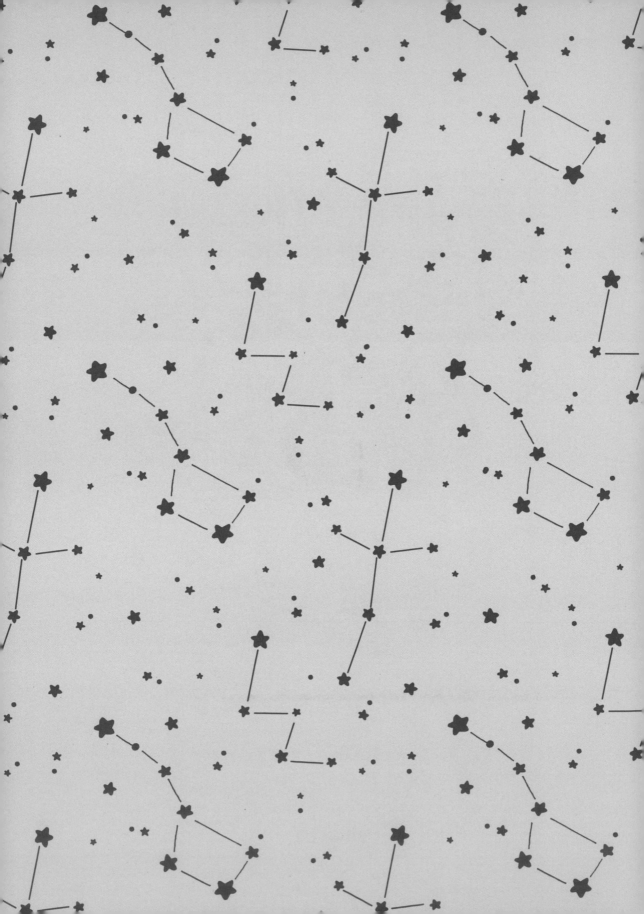

GOOD NIGHT STORIES FOR REBEL GIRLS 2

FRANCESCA CAVALLO AND ELENA FAVILLI

TIMBUKTU

Good Night Stories for Rebel Girls and *Good Night Stories for Rebel Girls 2* are available at special quantity discounts for bulk purchase for sale promotions, premiums, fundraising, and educational needs. For details, write to wholesale@rebelgirls.co.

Editorial Direction + Art Direction by Francesca Cavallo and Elena Favilli

Cover design by Pemberley Pond
Graphic design by Giulia Flamini

Editor: Anita Roy
Research Editor: Arianna Giorgia Bonazzi

Printed in Canada
Good Night Stories for Rebel Girls 2
is FSC certified. It is printed on
chlorine-free paper made with
30% post-consumer waste.
It uses only vegetable- and soy-based ink.

ENVIRONMENTAL BENEFITS STATEMENT

Timbuktu Labs Inc saved the following resources by printing the pages of this book on chlorine free paper made with 30% post-consumer waste.

TREES	WATER	ENERGY	SOLID WASTE	GREENHOUSE GASES
4,651 FULLY GROWN	2,174,215 GALLONS	2,090 MILLION BTUs	145,545 POUNDS	400,882 POUNDS

Environmental impact estimates were made using the Environmental Paper Network Paper Calculator 3.2. For more information visit www.papercalculator.org.

MIX
Paper from responsible sources
FSC® C016245
www.fsc.org

www.rebelgirls.co

FIRST EDITION
10 9 8 7 6 5 4 3 2 1

TO THE REBEL GIRLS
OF THE WORLD:

YOU ARE THE PROMISE
YOU ARE THE FORCE

DON'T STEP BACK,
AND EVERYONE
WILL MOVE FORWARD.

CONTENTS

Dearest Rebels,

As you read this letter, the first volume of *Good Night Stories for Rebel Girls* is on the nightstands of about one million people. All over the world, children and grown-ups are talking about their favorite rebel girl. Teachers are designing lessons around these pioneers. Politicians are reading these stories at political conventions, young women are opening the book to cheer up after a bad day, and soon-to-be dads are buying it to welcome their daughters into this world.

Good Night Stories for Rebel Girls has been translated into more than thirty languages, and every day we have the feeling that we hear all of your accents when we receive the messages you send us via email, Facebook, and Twitter. When we see the Instagram pictures of this book in your homes, it's a lot like looking at a family album. A family made up of people of every religion, every nationality, every color, every age, every kind. A global family whose members come from small villages (like the ones we grew up in) and from big cities.

One year ago, in our small Los Angeles apartment, we started a little fire. A fire we could gather around to tell each other new kinds of stories.

You joined us. You invited your friends and brought more firewood. You came bringing your hopes, your frustrations, your courage and your fear, your weakness and your strength. You came to listen, but you also came to speak. The fire got bigger. The family grew.

And this is what *Good Night Stories for Rebel Girls 2* is about. It's about the stories you told us by that fire. It's about the Asian American female firefighter whom Christine told us about in New York City. It's about the first all-female anti-poaching unit in South Africa, which Rita told us about on Snapchat. It's about the Irish pilot who built herself a plane. Aidan told us about her at a signing event.

Some say that stories can't change the world. But we disagree.

Time and again, you messaged us to say you had discovered a story in our book, and sometimes the story you mentioned wasn't there. The fact is that *Good Night Stories for Rebel Girls* is training hundreds of thousands of people to see stories they couldn't see before. It's inspiring them to look for talent where they thought there was none. It's making it easier to find potential in unpredictable places.

When we tap into the talent of an entire population—instead of just half of it—endless possibilities open up.

When we see each other for what we are, free of harmful stereotypes, we create real progress.

When we recognize oppression and take action to end it, we all become stronger.

As you rest your head on your pillow after reading one or three of these stories—whether it's after an exhausting day of play or a long day at work, whether you're in Cape Town or Aotearoa, whether someone read you the story or you read it by yourself—know that you've just sat by a fire with hundreds of thousands of fellow rebels who, just like you, are on a journey.

The Good Night Stories for Rebel Girls series is a small part of a conversation that is bigger than each of us. Bigger than our individual hopes. Certainly bigger than our fears.

Thank you for sitting with us by this fire.

Now let's get started.

Francesca Cavallo
Elena Favilli

AGATHA CHRISTIE

WRITER

Once upon a time, there was a girl who loved to write. Poems, love stories, mysteries, letters—she tried them all. Agatha wanted to be a professional writer more than anything. She talked about her dream with her dog, George Washington, during their daily walks. Each new place she and George visited, Agatha looked at as a setting for a story, and every time she met someone, she wondered if that person could be one of her characters.

Agatha sent her stories to magazines but got turned down. The rejection letters kept piling up, but Agatha didn't let that stop her. She was an avid reader and especially loved murder mysteries.

So she wrote her own detective novel.

The Mysterious Affair at Styles featured Hercule Poirot, a Belgian detective with a glorious mustache. Many publishers turned down Agatha's manuscript, but finally one said yes.

When the novel was published, it was a huge success and marked the beginning of an unbelievable career. Agatha Christie's books have sold more than two billion copies and have been translated into over a hundred different languages, making her the best-selling novelist of all time.

Hercule Poirot with his pointy mustache and Miss Marple with her cute hats became two of the most popular literary detectives ever. They appeared in TV shows and movies, and kept millions of people guessing as they figured out whodunnit.

Through her remarkable career, Agatha wrote sixty-six detective novels, fourteen short story collections, and the world's longest-running play, *The Mousetrap*.

SEPTEMBER 15, 1890–JANUARY 12, 1976
UNITED KINGDOM

"THE BEST TIME TO PLAN
A BOOK IS WHILE YOU'RE
DOING THE DISHES."
– AGATHA CHRISTIE

AISHOLPAN NURGAIV

EAGLE HUNTRESS

Once there was a thirteen-year-old girl named Aisholpan who lived in the icy-cold Altai Mountains. For seven generations, the men in her tribe had hunted with golden eagles to provide their families with food and fur.

Golden eagles are big, fierce creatures with sharp claws and curved beaks that can be extremely dangerous. But to Aisholpan, they were simply beautiful. She longed to train an eagle of her own, so one day she said to her father, "Dad, I know that no girls have ever done this, but if you teach me, I'll be good." Her father, who was a great eagle hunter, paused to think. Then he said, "You are strong. You are not afraid. You can do it."

Her heart sang with joy.

Aisholpan and her dad rode their horses high into the snowy mountains. Finding an eaglet to train wasn't easy. Aisholpan reached a nest with a rope tied around her waist, trying not to slip on the sharp rocks. In the nest, she found a tiny golden eagle, all alone.

She covered the bird's head with a blanket to calm her down, then brought her home. Aisholpan sang and told stories so that the eaglet would recognize her voice. She fed her small chunks of meat and taught her how to land on her glove. "I treat her with respect, because if she trusts me, she won't fly away. We will be a team for a few years. Then I'll return her to the wild. The circle of life must continue."

Aisholpan became the first woman to enter the Golden Eagle competition in Ölgii, Mongolia. After her, three more girls started training to become eagle hunters.

BORN 2003
MONGOLIA

4

ILLUSTRATION BY
SALLY NIXON

"I PLAN TO TEACH
MY YOUNGER SISTER
EAGLE HUNTING."
– AISHOLPAN NURGAIV

ALICE BALL

CHEMIST

Once upon a time, there was no cure for leprosy, a disease that attacks the body and can leave victims terribly disfigured. Because there was no treatment and people believed leprosy was very contagious, sufferers used to be isolated in leper colonies with nothing to do but wait for death—or for a cure to be found.

In search of that cure, an incredibly talented young Hawaiian chemist called Alice Ball was studying the properties of an oil extracted from the chaulmoogra tree. This oil was used in traditional Chinese and Indian medicine to treat skin diseases, and it also had been used for leprosy, with mixed results: sometimes it worked, and sometimes it didn't.

"Why?" was Alice's burning question. "Why doesn't it work *every* time?"

She teamed up with an assistant surgeon at a Honolulu hospital to try to find the answer to that question. She developed a way to separate out the active elements of chaulmoogra oil and created a new extract that could be injected directly into a patient's bloodstream—with amazing results.

Unfortunately, Alice died before she was able to publish her findings. So the University of Hawaii did it for her—without giving her credit! The president of the university even called the extraction technique the Dean Method, as if he had invented it himself.

Many years later, Alice Ball's amazing contribution was finally recognized. Now, every four years on February 29, Hawaii celebrates Alice Ball Day.

Alice was the first African American and the first woman to graduate from the University of Hawaii.

JULY 24, 1892-DECEMBER 31, 1916
UNITED STATES OF AMERICA

ILLUSTRATION BY
MARTINA PAUKOVA

ANDRÉE PEEL

FRENCH RESISTANCE FIGHTER

Once upon a time, there was a young woman who ran a beauty parlor. Andrée was smart and stylish, and she always had a bright smile for her customers. *"Bonjour, madame,"* she would call out. "How would you like your hair cut today?"

Then the Second World War broke out, and everything changed.

When Hitler invaded her country, Andrée joined the French Resistance, a network of ordinary people who worked in secret against the Nazis. She helped distribute underground newspapers to other members of the Resistance. It was risky and dangerous work. Andrée was soon promoted to sergeant and given the code name Agent Rose.

Many times she risked her life. She would steal out at night and line up a row of flaming torches to signal to Allied planes as they crossed enemy lines. The pilots looked for these bright spots and knew that they could land safely there, thanks to Agent Rose. She helped save over a hundred British pilots from being captured by the Nazis before she herself was captured and sent to a concentration camp.

Sick, starving, and dressed in blue-and-white-striped pajamas, Andrée was lined up with other prisoners in front of a firing squad, about to be shot, when Allied troops arrived and and saved them.

Andrée was hailed as a hero. The president of the United States and the British prime minister both sent her letters to thank her for everything she had done. She went on to live a long life—but she always kept a scrap of that blue-and-white material to remind her of those terrible days, and to confirm that, as she said, "Miracles do exist."

FEBRUARY 3, 1905–MARCH 5, 2010
FRANCE

"I WAS DESTINED ALWAYS TO BE A FIGHTER."
– ANDRÉE PEEL

ANGELA MERKEL

CHANCELLOR

O nce upon a time, in Templin, Germany, there lived a seven-year-old girl called Angela. One Sunday, she was listening to her father's sermon in church when her mother started to cry.

"What's the matter?" Angela asked.

"They are going to build a wall," her mother said. "They want to seal off the border between East Germany and West Germany."

Angela was stunned. "Why would they build a wall?" she thought. "People should be free to go wherever they like." Not only would East Germans be stopped from going to the West, but they would be barred from listening to the news coming from the other side.

Every day, Angela would hide in the school washroom with a little radio and try to catch a station from the West. It was illegal to do this, but she didn't care: she wanted to know what was happening to her country.

When Angela grew up, she studied **quantum chemistry** and wanted to become a university professor. The secret police told her that she would be promoted only if she spied for them. Angela refused, and she never became a professor.

She was working as a researcher in a lab when the Berlin Wall was demolished. She called her mom and said, "I think we're free to go to the West." Indeed, they were.

Angela eventually became chancellor of Germany—a determined leader who knew the pain walls could cause and never wanted her people to be divided again.

BORN JULY 17, 1954
GERMANY

ILLUSTRATION BY
ELENIA BERETTA

"WHAT WE SEEK IS HARMONY
AMONG NATIONS. THAT WAS
AND REMAINS THE GREATEST GOAL
OF EUROPEAN UNITY."
– ANGELA MERKEL

ANITA GARIBALDI

REVOLUTIONARY

Once upon a time, there was a skilled horsewoman who loved freedom. Her name was Anita. Her country—Brazil—was going through a difficult time. An emperor ruled the country, and a group of rebels, called Ragamuffins, had started an uprising to replace him with politicians who would be voted in by ordinary Brazilians.

Anita believed in democracy, so even though she knew that the Ragamuffins had little chance of beating the mighty imperial army, she joined their fight.

One day, a bearded Italian man called Giuseppe Garibaldi walked into a café. Anita and Giuseppe looked at each other, fell instantly in love, and decided to travel together to wherever the battle was bloodiest.

Anita was seven months pregnant when things got ugly for the rebels. Giuseppe ordered a retreat, but Anita kept fighting, even after her horse was killed. Total chaos broke out, and the two lost sight of each other.

Anita was captured and told by imperial troops that Giuseppe was dead. Heartbroken, she asked permission to cross back into enemy territory, on foot, to look for his body. When she couldn't find him, she stole a horse and escaped, crossing a raging river by hanging on to the horse's tail so she wouldn't be swept away. She traveled for days until, exhausted, she reached a farm—and there she found Giuseppe!

The two hugged and kissed, ecstatic to be together for the birth of their first son, Menotti. The Ragamuffin War was just the first in a series of battles Anita and Giuseppe fought together. Eventually, her name came to symbolize freedom and courage all over the world.

AUGUST 30, 1821–AUGUST 4, 1849
BRAZIL

"DO NOT BE
AFRAID TO LIVE,
TO RUN AFTER DREAMS.
BE AFRAID TO STAND STILL."
– ANITA GARIBALDI

ANNE BONNY

PIRATE

Anne was a girl with wild red hair. She was scruffy and tough, and she used to hang out with pirates at the port taverns. When she grew up, she even married one called John Bonny.

Together they sailed to the Bahamas, but when John started spying on his fellow pirates for the British government, Anne left him and ran away with a pirate captain named John Rackham. "Calico Jack," as he was known, was famous for wearing flamboyant trousers made from striped **calico cloth**.

Anne's best friend was a dressmaker called Pierre. One day, they decided to rob a French merchant vessel that was passing by. They splashed blood on their sails, the ship's deck, and themselves. They put one of Pierre's dresses on a mannequin and splashed that with blood too.

By the light of the full moon, they sailed silently toward the French ship. When they were close enough for the other crew to see, Anne appeared next to the mannequin brandishing an axe.

Terrified, the sailors abandoned ship without a fight!

Anne also became friends with another woman pirate named Mary Read. Disguised as a man, Mary was part of the crew on a ship that Anne and Calico Jack had captured. Anne and Mary took charge of the ship, which was called the *Revenge*. They dressed sometimes as men and sometimes as women, and became inseparable.

When the British Navy ordered the crew of the *Revenge* to surrender, Anne and Mary fought back fiercely, but because their fellow sailors were drunk, they were quickly captured.

MARCH 8, 1702–APRIL 22, 1782
IRELAND

"FOLLOW ME AT YOUR OWN PERIL."
– ANNE BONNY

AUDREY HEPBURN

ACTRESS

Once upon a time, in Holland, there was a little girl named Audrey who ate tulips.

It wasn't because she loved flowers, though—it was because she was so hungry. Life in Holland during the Second World War was hard. There was never enough food on the table, and Audrey often felt the pangs of hunger in her empty stomach. Tulip bulbs didn't taste good, but they kept her from starving.

When Audrey was older, she moved to England and became a film actress. She was admired the world over for her elegant figure and her luminous beauty. Famous fashion designers flocked to her, and she became a style icon, known for her little black dress, long gloves, and diamond tiara. After her most famous film, *Breakfast at Tiffany's*, was released, the "Hepburn look" became so popular that women used to dress just like her. They would even visit the famous jewelry store in New York City to stand on the same spot she did.

But Audrey wanted to do more than just star in films and be admired for her clothes. She wanted to help others, especially poor and hungry children—children who were as hungry as she had once been. She dedicated her life to serving UNICEF, the same charity that had helped her when she was a girl during the war. She believed that no child should ever be so hungry she would have to eat flower bulbs.

When Audrey died, a new pure white tulip was named in her honor, to celebrate the wonderful work she did for UNICEF.

MAY 4, 1929 – JANUARY 20, 1993
BELGIUM

"AS YOU GROW OLDER, YOU WILL DISCOVER
THAT YOU HAVE TWO HANDS: ONE FOR HELPING
YOURSELF, THE OTHER FOR HELPING OTHERS."
– AUDREY HEPBURN

BEATRICE VIO

FENCER

Once upon a time, there was an Italian girl who was a formidable fencer. Her name was Beatrice, but everyone called her Bebe.

While she was in middle school, Bebe became very ill. By the time her parents got her to the hospital, she was fighting for her life. She had contracted meningitis, a severe illness that attacks the brain and spinal cord, and to save her, the doctors had to amputate her legs and her forearms.

Bebe was in the hospital for more than a hundred days. When she recovered from the surgery, she had one goal in mind: to go back to fencing. Nearly everyone told her it was impossible. But Bebe had a plan.

First, she relearned how to walk, shower, open windows, and brush her teeth. She even taught her classmates how to use her brand-new artificial limbs! Then she strapped her foil to her arm and started training again. As the only wheelchair fencer in the world without arms and legs, Bebe had to invent a technique that would work just for her. After a while, she was ready to try competing again.

In a few years, and with the help of two of the most famous fencing teachers in Italy, she became a champion. She won the World Cup in Canada, the European Championships in Italy, the World Championship in Hungary, and the gold medal at the Paralympics in Rio de Janeiro.

"To be special," Bebe says, "you need to turn your weakness into the thing you're most proud of."

BORN MARCH 4, 1997
ITALY

"I DON'T TAKE NO FOR AN ANSWER."
– BEATRICE VIO

ILLUSTRATION BY CRISTINA PORTOLANO

BEATRIX POTTER

WRITER AND ILLUSTRATOR

Once upon a time in London, there lived a girl who loved to paint animals. Beatrix spent all year looking forward to the summer holidays, when she and her little brother could escape the drab, gray city streets for the wild Highlands of Scotland.

As soon as she had unpacked her bags, Beatrix would gather up her paints and brushes, pull on her boots, and head outside. She sat so quietly that field mice would scamper past her and rabbits would hop up and nibble the grass at her feet. The squirrels got quite used to her sitting at the edge of the woods as they chased each other through the branches above her head.

When she was old enough, Beatrix left the city and moved to the countryside. One day, she sent a letter to a young friend of hers, a little boy called Noel. In the letter, she made up a story about a naughty rabbit in a smart blue jacket who steals vegetables from the garden next door and is chased by the farmer. Beatrix named him Peter, after her own pet rabbit. Noel loved the story and wanted more, so Beatrix kept writing to him, and even included pictures of Peter and his three siblings, Flopsy, Mopsy, and Cottontail. Eventually, she published the story as an illustrated book.

Millions of children came to love Beatrix Potter's books and her unforgettable characters, including Mrs. Tiggy-winkle, Squirrel Nutkin, and the two naughty mice, Tom Thumb and Hunca Munca. Her very first book, *The Tale of Peter Rabbit*, became one of the most popular children's stories of all time.

JULY 28, 1866 – DECEMBER 22, 1943
UNITED KINGDOM

"THERE IS SOMETHING DELICIOUS ABOUT WRITING THE FIRST WORDS OF A STORY. YOU NEVER QUITE KNOW WHERE THEY'LL TAKE YOU."
— BEATRIX POTTER

BEYONCÉ

SINGER, SONGWRITER, AND BUSINESSWOMAN

Beyoncé was six years old when her dad started selling people tickets to go to their house and see her sing and dance. When Beyoncé told her mom she wanted to create a band with her friends, her mom said, "Okay. I'll make your costumes." And so Destiny's Child was born.

Beyoncé was the queen of the band. She was driven, focused, and interested in learning as much as possible about every aspect of the music business.

At first, her dad was her manager. But when she decided she wanted to be in control of her career, Beyoncé asked him to step aside. Madonna, the great singer-songwriter, was her role model. Like Madonna, Beyoncé didn't *just* want to be a popular singer—she wanted to be a powerhouse. And that's what she became.

One song at a time, one album at a time, one concert at a time, Beyoncé forged her own path and became an inspiration to people around the world. She sang about freedom, about love, about independence, and about pain: both personal pain and social injustice. She inspired millions of black women to be proud of their culture, of their origins, of their own unique style.

When Beyoncé was asked to perform during the halftime show of the Super Bowl, the biggest sporting event in the United States, she entered the stadium leading an army of female dancers all dressed in black. With her compelling song "Formation," she dropped a black power anthem in front of one hundred million viewers.

Today, she is the most influential living pop star in the whole world.

BORN SEPTEMBER 4, 1981
UNITED STATES OF AMERICA

"OKAY, LADIES,
NOW LET'S
GET IN FORMATION."
– BEYONCÉ

BILLIE JEAN KING

TENNIS PLAYER

Once there was a formidable tennis player called Billie Jean. She was a great champion who won all the most important tennis tournaments of her day. But there was something she found profoundly bothersome. At the time, female players earned only a fraction of the prize money that male players made.

"Why should women put up with being paid less?" Billie Jean protested. "We sell the same number of tickets."

"That's just how it is," the tournament organizers replied.

"Do something about it," she said, "or I will **boycott** your tournament."

The tournament organizers laughed at her, but she wasn't joking. She got together with nine other female tennis players, and they created their own circuit with nineteen tournaments and many big sponsors.

The battle for equality in tennis had just begun.

"A woman's place is in the kitchen, not on the tennis court," proclaimed Bobby Riggs, a male tennis player who strongly believed that women were worth less than men.

"Oh, yeah?" said Billie Jean. "I'll show you."

They played each other in a historic match called the Battle of the Sexes. Thirty thousand people in the stadium and fifty million television viewers watched Billie Jean beat Riggs in straight sets.

Organizers of the US Open finally met her demand, making it the first major tennis tournament to offer equal prize money to men and women. Thanks to Billie Jean, today tennis is one of the few sports where female and male athletes have achieved equal pay in all the biggest tournaments.

BORN NOVEMBER 22, 1943
UNITED STATES OF AMERICA

"IF YOU'RE GOING TO MAKE AN ERROR,
MAKE A DOOZY, AND DON'T BE AFRAID
TO HIT THE BALL."
– BILLIE JEAN KING

THE BLACK MAMBAS

RANGERS

One day, a park warden named Craig put together an all-female team of rangers to stop poachers in the South African savanna. He called them the Black Mambas.

He recruited high school graduates from the communities surrounding the wildlife park. "It's important to protect the rhinos," he explained, "so future generations will see them for real and not just on posters!" He gave the women uniforms and set up a training program.

The Black Mambas learned how to survive in the savanna, how to spot animal traps, and what to do when they encountered lions, elephants, buffaloes, and hyenas. They learned how to track poachers and patrol the park's perimeter fence—armed with only pepper spray and handcuffs.

"This war on poaching is bigger than guns and bullets," declared Nomutu Magakene, one of the Mambas. "We are the eyes and ears of the reserves. We're doing things differently."

The Black Mambas took great pride in their work. They talked to people about the importance of rhinos in their communities, and about how lucky they were to live in one of the most biodiverse countries in the world. They gave presentations in schools and taught children that it was wrong to cooperate with poachers and lay traps in the park.

They became heroes.

"To be a Black Mamba means to be a tough and strong lady," said Nomutu, "one who can work in the bushes without fear."

It took only a year of Black Mamba patrols for the snaring to disappear almost completely and the rhino killings to stop entirely.

STARTED 2007
SOUTH AFRICA

ILLUSTRATION BY
ALICE BENIERO

"WE ARE FIGHTING FOR OUR ANIMALS AND SHOWING PEOPLE
THAT WOMEN CAN BE BEAUTIFUL AND STRONG."
— LEITAH

BOUDICCA

QUEEN

Once upon a time, there was a fearless warrior queen who spearheaded a rebellion against the Romans.

Boudicca was just twenty-eight years old when she led her tribe, the Iceni, into battle. Her husband, the king, had died and left his kingdom to her. But the Roman emperor, Nero, decided that no woman could rule an area under Roman control, and he sent his troops to enslave the Britons. The noble Iceni were killed or imprisoned, their queen was made to walk naked in the street, and her daughters were whipped.

Boudicca wanted revenge for this humiliating treatment. She gathered together a tribal army and led an attack against the mighty Roman Empire. With her long red hair flying and her sword held high over her head, she struck fear into the hearts of her enemies. Her army stormed the city of Colchester, in southeastern England, destroying the temple of Claudius, the former Roman emperor, and killing thousands of Romans and their supporters.

Even more Britons joined Boudicca, and by the time she reached London, her army was a hundred thousand strong—all of them loyal to the rebel queen. But despite being heavily outnumbered, the Romans, who had better weapons, won and Boudicca died fighting.

Her name comes from the Celtic word *bouda*, meaning "victory." For her bravery and her strength, she came to symbolize the fighting spirit of the British. Today, you can still see a huge bronze statue of Boudicca and her daughters, driving a magnificent horse-drawn carriage, in London, near Westminster Bridge.

C. 33-61

UNITED KINGDOM

ILLUSTRATION BY
MONICA GARWOOD

"I AM NOT FIGHTING FOR
MY KINGDOM AND WEALTH NOW.
I AM FIGHTING AS AN
ORDINARY PERSON
FOR MY LOST FREEDOM,
MY BRUISED BODY, AND
MY OUTRAGED DAUGHTERS."
– BOUDICCA

～ BRENDA MILNER ～

NEUROPSYCHOLOGIST

B renda wanted to understand how the brain works, so she studied psychology at Cambridge University.

After college, she moved to Canada and pursued her PhD at the Montreal Neurological Institute. She was such a good student that she was offered a position as a professor at McGill University, but much to everyone's astonishment, she turned it down.

Her colleagues told her, "You're a psychologist in a neurological institute. This is no place to build your career." And Brenda answered, simply, "I like it here."

Shortly after, she was asked to work with a special patient who had undergone surgery to remove the temporal lobes on both sides of his brain, making it impossible for him to create new long-term memories.

Every day, Brenda would sit with the man, running different tests and taking detailed notes. Eventually, she started to notice something strange: each morning, her patient showed improvement on all the tests, even though he had no memory of doing them the day before. It was a groundbreaking discovery! Brenda realized that the brain has at least two different memory systems: one that handles names, faces, and experiences, and a second that handles motor skills, such as swimming or playing the piano.

"It was the most exciting moment of my life," she recalled.

Brenda would sit with patients, talk to them, and write down every tiny detail they told her. In this way, she was able to detect specific brain injuries.

Brenda is considered the founder of neuropsychology and one of the world's leading experts on memory.

BORN JULY 15, 1918
UNITED KINGDOM

"I AM INCREDIBLY
CURIOUS ABOUT THE
LITTLE THINGS I SEE
AROUND ME."
– BRENDA MILNER

BUFFALO CALF ROAD WOMAN

WARRIOR

Once upon a time, there was a girl who saved her brother during a battle. She was Cheyenne, and her name was Buffalo Calf Road Woman.

At the time, settlers and government soldiers were determined to steal the land from the Native Americans who were its original inhabitants. As General George Crook led his troops across the Great Plains toward her village, Buffalo Calf Road Woman took her gun, leapt onto her horse, and joined the Cheyenne men to fight back. Some of them protested that because she was a woman, she couldn't take part in the fight, but she had already pushed her horse into a gallop, a cloud of dust billowing behind her.

The battle was raging when she suddenly spotted her brother, Comes in Sight, trapped in a gully and surrounded by Crook's soldiers. Fearlessly, Buffalo Calf Road Woman sprinted down the ditch with bullets flying all around. She pulled her brother onto her horse, and they galloped off together to safety. It was a breathtaking rescue.

The other warriors couldn't believe their eyes. They hadn't been nearly as brave as Buffalo Calf Road Woman. If it hadn't been for her, Comes in Sight would have been killed.

They felt diminished by her courage and didn't want anyone to know what had happened, so they agreed never to talk about her feat. But one valiant warrior called Wooden Leg spoke up. It's because of him that today we know the wonderful story of one of the bravest warriors in the West, Buffalo Calf Road Woman.

C. 1850s–MAY 1879
UNITED STATES OF AMERICA

ILLUSTRATION BY
ANA JUAN

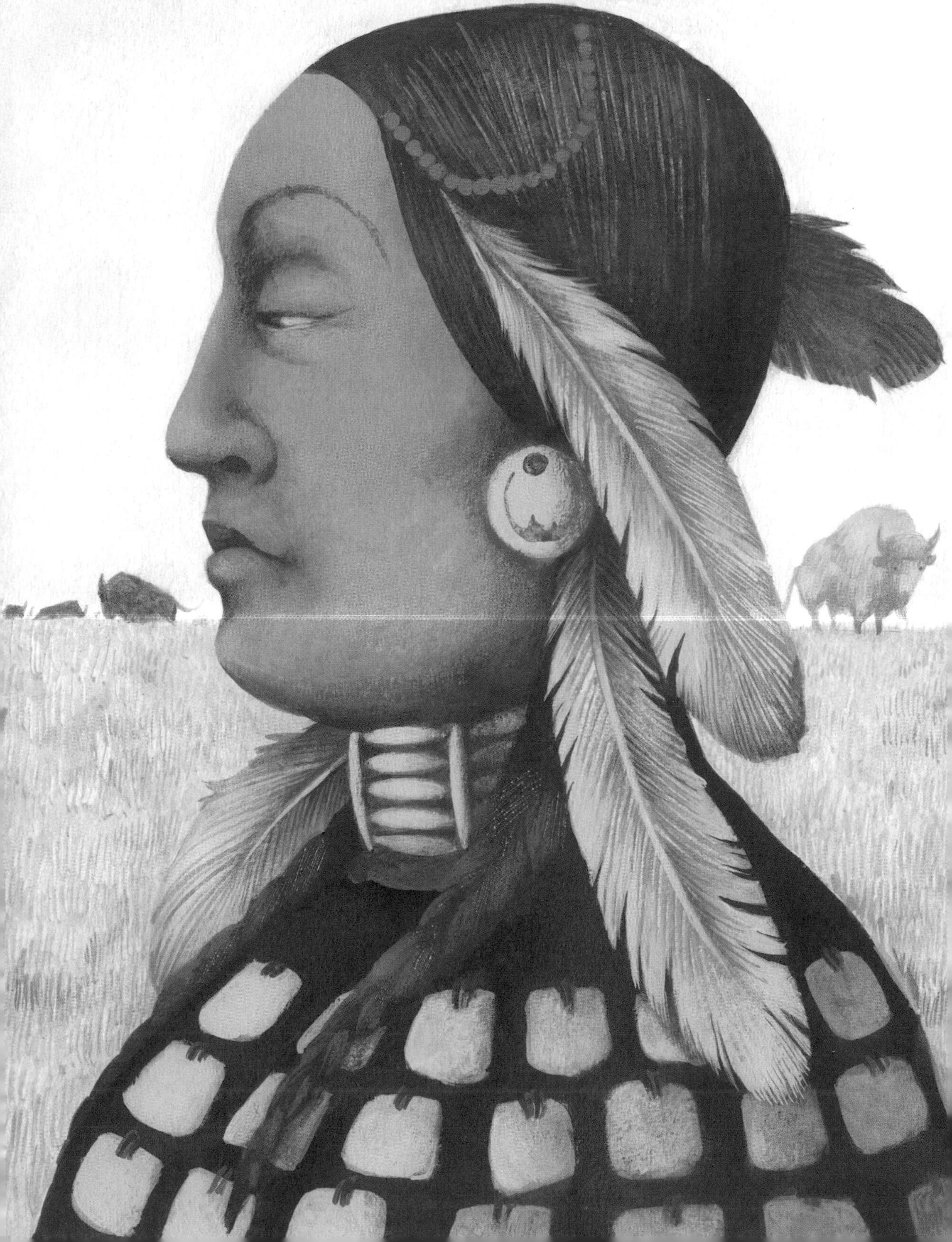

MADAM C.J. WALKER

BUSINESSWOMAN

Once upon a time, on a cotton plantation in Louisiana, a girl named Sarah was born. Sarah's four older siblings had been born into slavery, as had their parents before them. But thanks to an important law called the Emancipation Proclamation, Sarah was the first in her family to be born free.

When Sarah was fourteen, she moved to St. Louis, Missouri. There, she worked as a washerwoman for $1.50 a day. At night, she attended school.

During that time, Sarah started losing her hair, so she experimented with various products and treatments to help it grow back again. None of the available products was quite right for her, however. "What if I could create a hair treatment specifically for African Americans?" she wondered.

Her husband, who worked in advertising, loved the idea. He suggested she change her name to "Madam" C.J. Walker to make her products more appealing, and so she did.

Sarah started traveling the country to promote her hair care line and gave demonstrations of the Walker System: a hair care formula that used homemade pomade (a scented oil), heated combs, and a particular style of brushing to stimulate hair growth. Her demonstrations were so popular, she started hiring other women to promote her products, and soon "Walker agents" became well known all over the country.

Sarah's success encouraged other women to create their own companies, and she supported many charities providing educational opportunities for African Americans.

Madam C.J. Walker became the first female self-made millionaire in America.

DECEMBER 23, 1867–MAY 25, 1919
UNITED STATES OF AMERICA

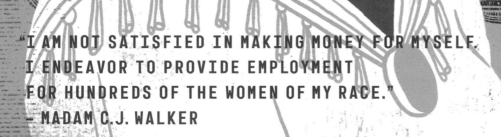

"I AM NOT SATISFIED IN MAKING MONEY FOR MYSELF.
I ENDEAVOR TO PROVIDE EMPLOYMENT
FOR HUNDREDS OF THE WOMEN OF MY RACE."
– MADAM C.J. WALKER

CARMEN AMAYA

DANCER

The night Carmen Amaya came into the world, Barcelona was lashed by a terrible storm. Thunder boomed, lightning crashed, and the rain turned the narrow lanes into raging streams of filthy water.

Carmen's family were Romany gypsies, and flamenco dancing was in their blood. When Carmen's father first saw her dance, he wondered if something of that storm had entered his daughter's veins when she was born.

Carmen learned flamenco steps from her aunt, who was herself a great dancer. But the little girl never played by the rules: she made up her own. To earn money, she danced barefoot in the *tavernas* down by the waterfront. She gained the respect of even the toughest sailors, who nicknamed her La Capitana—the Captain.

Soon she began to perform in big theaters. She earned enough money for her family to move out of the shack where she was born and into a decent apartment. They could afford to eat ham sandwiches instead of sardines.

Onstage, Carmen preferred tight-fitting trousers and a high-cut bolero jacket to the *traje de flamenca*, the traditional dress worn by female dancers. When she first appeared like that, the audience was in an uproar. How dare this slip of a girl wear men's clothing! But when she began to dance, Carmen silenced them all. Stamping out lightning-fast rhythms on the stage, she sometimes broke the floorboards. Her footwork was so ferocious, said one member of the audience, "her dancing was almost supernatural."

Carmen was such an incredible dancer that to this day, she is remembered as the Queen of the Gypsies.

NOVEMBER 2, 1918 – NOVEMBER 19, 1963
SPAIN

"TROUSERS ARE
UNFORGIVING: THEY SHOW
UP EVERY MISTAKE AND
THEY GIVE YOU NOTHING
TO TAKE HOLD OF."
– CARMEN AMAYA

CELIA CRUZ

SINGER

Once, in the poor quarter of Havana, Cuba, a young girl used to sing her brothers and sisters to sleep. "What an incredible voice!" said the neighbors. "She sings like an angel."

When Celia was older, her cousin entered her in a singing competition on a local radio station. She came first—and won a cake as a prize!

Celia loved to sing **Santeria** songs in the Yoruba language of West Africa. Her father disapproved of her singing and wanted her to become a teacher. But music, and especially the bewitching rhythms of **salsa**, ran through Celia's veins.

She joined the National Conservatory of Music and started to make recordings. One day, a popular salsa band called La Sonora Matancera needed a new singer. This was Celia's big break—and she leapt at the chance.

But soon after, a revolution broke out in Cuba, and many musicians fled to the United States. Celia was one of them. Still, she never forgot where she came from.

One day, when she was at a café in Miami, a waiter asked her if she took her coffee with or without sugar. "Are you crazy?" she laughed. "I'm Cuban! We *always* have *azúcar*!" From then on, whenever she was onstage, she would cry out, "*Azúcar!*"—"Sugar!"—and the crowd would go wild.

With her flamboyant personality, her amazing voice, and her infectious rhythms, Celia helped to make salsa music wildly popular in America. She recorded more than seventy albums, won several Grammy Awards, and was the undisputed Queen of Salsa for forty years.

OCTOBER 21, 1925 – JULY 16, 2003
CUBA

"OH, NO NEED TO CRY, LIFE IS A CARNIVAL."
— CELIA CRUZ

CHIMAMANDA NGOZI ADICHIE

WRITER

Once upon a time in Nigeria, there was a little girl called Chimamanda who loved books. She read all the books she could find, and when she was seven years old, she started to write her own stories.

Chimamanda had always lived in Nigeria. She snacked on mangoes and played in the sun all year long. Still, all the characters in her stories were white: they had blue eyes, ate apples, and played in the snow. "I didn't think people with chocolate-colored skin could be in books," she said.

One day, Chimamanda realized that was a silly thought and started to look for African books with African people in them. Even though she lived in Africa, these were harder to find than European or American books full of white people. But when she did, she thought it was great to see people who looked like her as characters in books. She wanted to see more of them.

Chimamanda became an exceptional writer. She traveled the world and told stories about Nigeria and America, about women and men, about migration and hair salons, about fashion and war.

She had a witty sense of humor and an amazing gift for explaining apparently complicated things clearly. People loved her books. They loved her speeches. They shared videos of her lectures with one another to feel inspired and empowered.

Chimamanda became a passionate advocate for gender equality. "Some people say women should be subordinate to men because it's our culture," she said. "But culture is constantly changing! Culture does not make people. People make culture!"

BORN SEPTEMBER 15, 1977
NIGERIA

"RACISM SHOULD NEVER HAVE
HAPPENED AND SO YOU DON'T GET
A COOKIE FOR REDUCING IT."
– CHIMAMANDA NGOZI ADICHIE

CHRISTINA OF SWEDEN

QUEEN

Once upon a time, there was a six-year-old queen. Her name was Christina, and she had succeeded her father on the throne upon his death.

Christina was smart and fiercely independent. Because she had a lot of responsibility on her shoulders, she knew she had to grow up fast, so she studied philosophy, art, foreign languages—and even ballet, to be able to move as gracefully as a queen.

When Christina turned eighteen, everyone expected her to marry a suitable man from a noble family—someone to increase her power. But she was in love with one of her ladies-in-waiting, a young and beautiful woman called Ebba Sparre, and she had no interest in marriage.

After reigning for ten years, Christina shocked everyone by giving up the throne and moving to Rome. There, she had a wonderful time, making friends with artists, writers, scientists, and musicians from all over Europe. She realized that she missed being queen, however, and plotted to seize control of the Kingdom of Naples, but her plan quickly fell apart.

Pope Alexander II called her "a queen without a realm, a Christian without faith, and a woman without shame," and he was right. Christina was never ashamed to show the world who she really was, even in the face of criticism. She was unconventional and she loved it. Thanks to her free spirit, she became one of the most influential women of her times.

In Rome, Christina formed the literary circle that gave rise to the Academy of Arcadia, an institute for literature and philosophy that exists to this day.

DECEMBER 8, 1626–APRIL 19, 1689
SWEDEN

"IT IS A FAR GREATER HAPPINESS
TO OBEY NO ONE THAN TO RULE THE WHOLE WORLD."
– CHRISTINA OF SWEDEN

CLARA ROCKMORE

MUSICIAN

One day, in Russia, a four-year-old girl stood on a table and started playing the violin. Her name was Clara, and she was auditioning for the St. Petersburg Conservatory.

Clara was a child prodigy, and she had her heart set on becoming a famous violinist.

After the Russian Revolution, though, Clara's parents decided to flee the country. They undertook a difficult and dangerous journey that was partly paid for by concerts given by Clara and her sister along the way. By the time they reached New York City, Clara had developed a weakness in her arm that forced her to abandon the violin. She was heartbroken.

Before long, however, Clara saw something miraculous: an instrument that could be played without being touched at all! The performer stood in front of an electronic deck and waved her hands between two antennas. Her movements were picked up by the device and transmitted as music, like a magician weaving a spell. This strange new instrument was called a theremin, for its inventor, Leon Theremin.

"I can play in the air," said Clara. "It is so beautiful!"

The theremin was hard to play, but she was a natural. She became a pioneer of electronic music and the world's most famous theremist. Her hands floated over the theremin, and the sweetest, most enchanting melodies materialized out of thin air.

Leon Theremin fell in love with Clara. He made her a birthday cake that spun and lit up as soon as she got close to it. He proposed to her many times, but Clara never married him.

MARCH 9, 1911 – MAY 10, 1998
LITHUANIA

ILLUSTRATION BY
CRISTINA SPANÓ

"I WAS FASCINATED BY THE
IDEA OF PLAYING IN THE AIR."
— CLARA ROCKMORE

CLARA SCHUMANN

PIANIST AND COMPOSER

By the time Clara was eight years old, she was already an extraordinary pianist.

After one of her concerts in a private home, she was approached by a seventeen-year-old boy: his name was Robert Schumann, and he was a pianist too. He told Clara that she was fantastic, and the two were soon good friends.

Clara traveled throughout Europe giving concerts, and she became one of the most famous composers and pianists of her time. Robert was also a great composer, and their shared love of music brought the two closer and closer, until they married when Clara was twenty-one.

At the time, female musicians were expected to stop working after marriage; some people believed that composing music would take away the energy needed to deliver and raise children. But for Clara, playing and composing music was not just a job: it was her passion, her skill, her reason for living. She had no intention of giving it up.

She and Robert eventually had seven children, and Clara gave hundreds of concerts—more than any other contemporary pianist! She also composed more than twenty piano works, a concerto, chamber music, and several shorter songs.

Clara and Robert loved each other dearly, and when he died, she stopped composing and devoted her life to playing his music to audiences around the world. Years later, as she herself lay dying, she asked her nephew to play the Romance in F Sharp Major, a piece Robert had composed for her. She died before the last notes had faded away.

SEPTEMBER 13, 1819–MAY 20, 1896
GERMANY

"IF I HAVE KNOWN
MUCH TROUBLE IN MY YOUTH,
I HAVE ALSO KNOWN MUCH JOY."
– CLARA SCHUMANN

CLEMANTINE WAMARIYA

STORYTELLER AND ACTIVIST

"Once upon a time" was Clemantine's favorite phrase. Every night, she would listen to the magical stories her nanny told her. Every morning, she would go to kindergarten. Every afternoon, she would come home to play under the mango tree, and every evening she would have dinner with her family. She was a happy child.

One day, though, her beloved nanny disappeared. Shortly after, Clemantine stopped going to kindergarten. Then her parents forbid her to play outside. Then they all moved into the smallest room of their house, and they kept the lights off at night.

Finally, Clemantine's parents put her and her sister, Claire, in a car so they could be driven to their grandma's.

Six-year-old Clemantine and nine-year-old Claire arrived safely, but after two days, their grandma told them that they had to run. The same people who had made their nanny disappear were now looking for them.

The sisters walked for days, weeks, and months. Clemantine didn't know where she was or why her parents weren't there.

After spending seven years on and off in African refugee camps, Claire and Clemantine eventually arrived in Chicago to start a new life. Clemantine went back to school, where she studied history and learned about the **Rwandan genocide**. She came to understand that in the world, there are many children who, like her and Claire, have been displaced and have lost their families.

She became a storyteller and an activist. Through her stories, she helps refugees cultivate courage, resilience, and hope, even in the middle of chaos.

BORN DECEMBER 18, 1988
RWANDA

"SAFETY SHOULD BE
A BIRTHRIGHT."
– CLEMANTINE WAMARIYA

CORRIE TEN BOOM

WATCHMAKER

Once upon a time, a girl named Corrie was born in a watch shop in Haarlem, Netherlands. Corrie's grandfather had been a watchmaker, as had her father, and when Corrie grew up, she decided to follow family tradition and became the first licensed female watchmaker in Holland.

But making watches wasn't the only family tradition Corrie followed. The ten Booms were devout Christians who believed in opening their house to anyone in need. So when Jews started being persecuted during the Second World War, Corrie knew she needed to help.

She built a secret room behind a false wall in her bedroom, and she joined a network called the Dutch underground, which protected people being hunted by the Nazis. Corrie installed a buzzer to signal danger. Every time soldiers came to search the shop, she would ring the buzzer and the people hiding in her house would have about a minute to disappear into the secret room.

One day, a Dutch informant betrayed Corrie and sent the Nazi secret police, known as the Gestapo, to raid her home. They found evidence that she had been helping Jews and members of the Dutch underground, and they arrested her and her father. But they were unable to find the secret room, where six people were hiding.

Corrie and her father were sent to prison for almost a year.

They saved more than eight hundred Jews, as well as many members of the Dutch underground. Corrie became a symbol of courage, unity, and unwavering dignity for people from all religious backgrounds and walks of life.

APRIL 15, 1892 - APRIL 15, 1983
THE NETHERLANDS

ILLUSTRATION BY
CLAUDIA CARIERI

TEN BOOM HORLOGERIE
HAARLEM
1837

"THE MEASURE
OF A LIFE,
AFTER ALL,
IS NOT
ITS DURATION,
BUT ITS DONATION."
– CORRIE TEN BOOM

ELEANOR ROOSEVELT

POLITICIAN

Once there was a serious girl called Eleanor Roosevelt.

When she was a teenager, Eleanor was sent to school in London. There, she met an extraordinary teacher named Marie Souvestre. Ms. Souvestre wanted Eleanor to think for herself, to be free and independent. Eleanor studied with her for three years, then she was summoned home because her grandmother wanted her to get married.

Back in the United States, Eleanor met another Roosevelt. His name was Franklin Delano. They got married, but soon after, he contracted polio. The disease left him paralyzed from the waist down, but Eleanor didn't let him give up on his dreams. With her determination and support, he went on to become the president of the United States.

As first lady, Eleanor gave speeches, traveled throughout all the states, and became a champion for human rights. She believed that all human beings are born free and equal in dignity and rights, and she was determined to promote those rights in as many countries as possible.

After her husband died, Eleanor was named the US delegate to the United Nations. She became the chairperson of the Commission on Human Rights and led the creation of one of the most important documents of the twentieth century: the Universal Declaration of Human Rights.

This beautiful document inspired governments to pass laws protecting human life and encouraged citizens to take action when their fundamental rights were denied. Thanks to Eleanor—and to the tireless work of many representatives from all over the world—freedom, equality, dignity, respect, and safety became common goals for all people and all nations.

OCTOBER 11, 1884–NOVEMBER 7, 1962
UNITED STATES OF AMERICA

THE UNIVERSAL DECLARATION
OF HUMAN RIGHTS

"DO ONE THING EVERY DAY
THAT SCARES YOU."
– ELEANOR ROOSEVELT

ELLEN DEGENERES

COMEDIAN AND TV HOST

One night, Ellen dreamt of a bird in a cage. In the dream, the bird realized that there was enough space between the bars to fly away.

Ellen knew exactly what the dream meant. She was a comedian, and she starred in a popular TV show where she played a woman who loved men. In reality, though, Ellen loved women. But she couldn't tell anybody.

At the time, her bosses thought that if the show's fans knew she was a lesbian, they would stop watching. But keeping silent didn't feel right to Ellen. She didn't want to hide anymore, and she wanted other gay people across the world to see that they were not alone. So in one of the episodes of her show, her character came out to her therapist, who was played by Oprah Winfrey. It was the first time in history that a lead character on a television program was openly gay. Next, Ellen told the public that she too was gay.

Her revelation sent shock waves through American media. Her show was eventually canceled, and Ellen found herself jobless and depressed. For three years, she didn't receive any offers of work.

Then one day, the phone rang. "Would you like to play a fish with memory issues in a new Pixar movie?" the caller asked. Ellen was ecstatic. The fish—named Dory—became an iconic character.

Today, Ellen is a superstar. She received the Presidential Medal of Freedom for her courage, and her talk show is watched every day by millions of people. "Find out who you are and figure out what you believe in," she likes to say. "Even if it's different from what your neighbors believe in and different from what your parents believe in."

BORN JANUARY 26, 1958
UNITED STATES OF AMERICA

"PEOPLE ALWAYS ASK ME,
WERE YOU FUN
AS A CHILD? NO,
I WAS AN ACCOUNTANT."
– ELLEN DEGENERES

FLORENCE CHADWICK

SWIMMER

The ocean was Florence's favorite place. Her parents would watch her from the beach as she swam and swam and swam. She was such a strong swimmer that everyone expected her to be chosen to compete in the Olympic Games in Los Angeles.

But Florence didn't like swimming pools. She thought they were boring. She loved feeling the cold water of the sea, reading the currents, watching for sharks, finding her rhythm with the waves. She loved to swim into the unknown. "In open water," she said, "you never know which fish you might encounter, or how the conditions might change."

Even though she could swim farther than almost anyone else, man or woman, Florence wasn't considered a professional athlete. Professional swimmers swam only in pools, and Florence still didn't like pools. So she took a job as a secretary in Saudi Arabia. Whenever she wasn't working, she was out swimming in the Persian Gulf. She saved every penny she could, because she had one goal in mind: "One day, I will swim across the English Channel."

When she was ready, Florence used all her savings to buy her dad a plane ticket from California to France. She hired a boat so he could follow her during the Channel crossing, encourage her, and give her snacks along the way. It was still night when she jumped in the water and started to swim.

Florence became the first woman to swim across the English Channel in both directions, as well as the first woman to swim the Strait of Gibraltar, the Bosporus, and the Dardanelles. Sometimes she failed, but she never stopped looking for new channels to cross.

NOVEMBER 9, 1918 - MARCH 15, 1995
UNITED STATES OF AMERICA

ILLUSTRATION BY
NOA SNIR

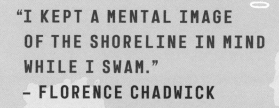

"I KEPT A MENTAL IMAGE
OF THE SHORELINE IN MIND
WHILE I SWAM."
– FLORENCE CHADWICK

GAE AULENTI

ARCHITECT AND DESIGNER

Once there was a girl who couldn't stand seeing ruins. The Second World War had destroyed her school and all the other places she loved. "One day, I'll rebuild everything," she promised herself. Her name was Gae.

When the war finally ended, Gae studied to be an architect. At the time, architecture was a field dominated by men, and she was one of only two women in a class of fifty.

But Gae wasn't easily intimidated. After graduating, she became one of the few female architects involved in rebuilding Italy after the war.

Gae saw architecture as a way to manipulate space with light. When she was asked to transform the old Gare d'Orsay railway station in Paris into a museum, she allowed natural light to flood into the huge main hall through a ceiling of glass. For an Olivetti showroom in Buenos Aires, Argentina, she used typewriters and mirrors to create a flight of steps seemingly multiplying into infinity.

Gae also worked as a theatrical set designer. "Theater taught me the value of action for architecture," she once said. "In architecture, a door is just a door. But onstage, a door can be a border, a crossing."

She constantly experimented with furniture and everyday objects. She designed a movable table using four bicycle wheels to hold up a floating glass top. For her iconic Pipistrello lamp, she created a lampshade shaped like the wings of a bat.

Gae worked her entire life designing buildings, museums, objects, and public spaces all over the world. She is regarded as one of the greatest architects of all time.

DECEMBER 4, 1927 - OCTOBER 31, 2012

ITALY

ILLUSTRATION BY
GAIA STELLA

"DURING THE DAY,
A WINDOW IS A
BEAUTIFUL LAMP."
— GAE AULENTI

GEORGIA O'KEEFFE

PAINTER

Once upon a time, a woman saw a door. It was an ordinary door, weathered and old and set into an adobe mud wall. But the woman was no ordinary woman. Her name was Georgia O'Keeffe, and she was a great artist.

She spent the whole day making a painting of the door. Then she stepped back and looked at the canvas. There was something not quite right, something missing. So she started another painting. This one was better than the first, she decided, but it still wasn't quite right. She started again. And again. She made over twenty paintings of the same door!

Every time Georgia set out to paint something, she wanted to get at the heart of whatever it was—a flower, a hillside, an animal skull, or an ordinary old door. She wanted to paint not just what a flower *looked* like, but what it *was*; its very essence.

"When you take a flower and really look at it," she explained, "it's your world for the moment." Her paintings of flowers were huge—it was as though one flower could fill the entire sky. With simple shapes and blocks of color, Georgia created a whole new language of art.

Her work became hugely popular, and everyone wanted to meet her. But Georgia liked being on her own. She lived in a place called Ghost Ranch in New Mexico. She loved it there, where the desert light was strong and clear, and the landscape was wild and free—just like her.

NOVEMBER 15, 1887 - MARCH 6, 1986
UNITED STATES OF AMERICA

"TO CREATE ONE'S OWN WORLD TAKES COURAGE."
– GEORGIA O'KEEFFE

GERTY CORI

BIOCHEMIST

Once upon a time, there was a girl who was named after a warship. Gerty was sixteen years old when she decided she wanted to study science. She was told she couldn't, however, because she didn't have enough background in Latin, mathematics, physics, and chemistry. But Gerty didn't give up: in one year, she managed to study the equivalent of eight years of Latin and five years of math, physics, and chemistry.

She was one of the first women to be admitted to the medical school at Charles University in Prague. There, Gerty became close friends with a fellow student called Carl Cori. He loved her charm, her sense of humor, and her passion for mountain climbing. They graduated, got married, immigrated to the United States, and stayed happily together for the rest of their lives.

In the United States, Gerty and Carl worked side by side in a laboratory and collaborated on scientific papers. Together they discovered how **glucose** is broken down by **enzymes** in the body to release energy. This process came to be known as the Cori cycle.

Their research has helped thousands of children with **diabetes**, and it also won them a Nobel Prize in Physiology or Medicine. Gerty was the first American woman to win a Nobel Prize in a scientific discipline, and the Coris were one of the very few married couples to win the prize jointly.

Theirs was a true partnership of equals. Gerty and Carl worked together on their scientific research to the end of their lives. When she was asked what was the secret to true happiness, Gerty replied: "The love for and dedication to one's work."

AUGUST 15, 1896 – OCTOBER 26, 1957
CZECH REPUBLIC

"I BELIEVE THAT IN ART
AND SCIENCE ARE
THE GLORIES OF THE
HUMAN MIND. I SEE
NO CONFLICT
BETWEEN THEM."
– GERTY CORI

GIUSI NICOLINI

MAYOR

There was a young woman named Giusi who loved the little island of Lampedusa, where she was born. Criminal groups and ruthless corporations wanted to destroy Lampedusa's pristine beaches to build hotels and vacation homes, but Giusi wouldn't let them.

As the director of Lampedusa's natural reserve, she said, "It is my duty to protect this island with all my might." Her enemies burned down her father's shop. "You will not intimidate me," she declared. Her car and her boyfriend's van were set on fire. "I will not back down!"

Lampedusa is a tiny island in the Mediterranean Sea, between Europe and Africa. Many refugees who were fleeing Africa to escape war and build a better life in Europe landed there. The inhabitants of Lampedusa didn't know what to do. "Should we send these people back to protect our island?" they wondered. "Or should we welcome them?"

With these questions in mind, they went to vote for their next mayor. Giusi was one of five candidates. People knew she had given all she had to protect the island in the past, so they wanted to hear what she thought about the current situation. Giusi explained her point of view with four simple words: "Protect people, not borders."

Lampedusans elected her.

As mayor, Giusi reorganized the island's immigration center to be able to welcome as many people as possible. "We want to see many boats on our shores," she insisted, "because that will mean that these people made it here and didn't drown."

BORN MARCH 5, 1961
ITALY

"I PLEDGE THIS AWARD
TO ALL THOSE WHO
DID NOT MANAGE
TO CROSS THE SEA
BECAUSE THEY
ENDED UP
BENEATH IT."
– GIUSI NICOLINI

GLORIA STEINEM

ACTIVIST

Once upon a time, there was a woman who traveled a lot. When she was a child, she traveled in her parents' trailer. When she grew up, she kept traveling by plane, train, bus—even on the back of an elephant! She traveled tens of thousands of miles, year after year, because she had an important message to spread and she wanted to deliver it in person to as many people as possible.

Her name was Gloria Steinem, and her message was simple yet revolutionary: she believed that women and men should be equal. She believed that women should have the right to decide if they want children, that their salaries should be the same as men's, and that they should never have to suffer abuse from their husbands.

Gloria was a feminist.

Many people thought a woman without a man wasn't really a complete person. Gloria thought that was ridiculous. "A woman without a man," she joked, "is like a fish without a bicycle!"

She told women that they could choose whatever life they wanted, and that not everyone had to live the same way. They didn't have to have children if they didn't want to. She also believed that people form families in many different ways, and that any family can be happy—as long as everyone in it loves and respects one another.

To this day, Gloria inspires women all over the world to fight for their rights. "Sometimes, the truth can make you mad," she admits, "but it will ultimately set you free."

BORN MARCH 25, 1934
UNITED STATES OF AMERICA

ILLUSTRATION BY
MALIN ROSENQVIST

"POWER CAN BE TAKEN,
BUT NOT GIVEN.
THE PROCESS OF THE TA
IS EMPOWERMENT IN ITS
– GLORIA STEINEM

HEDY LAMARR

ACTRESS AND INVENTOR

O nce upon a time, in Austria, a beautiful baby girl called Hedy was born. When Hedy grew up, she married a rich man and moved to a castle. At first, it seemed like a dream come true, but Hedy soon discovered that she and her husband didn't get along. "I was like a doll," she said. "He thought I had no mind!" What's more, her husband sold weapons to Nazis and fascists, and she often had to sit in meetings about military technologies that would be used to advance the agendas of these evil regimes.

One day, Hedy decided she'd had enough, so she disguised herself as a maid and escaped to Paris. There, she met an important Hollywood producer called Louis B. Mayer. She followed him to Los Angeles and eventually made eighteen movies, becoming one of the world's biggest film stars.

In between movies, Hedy invented a new kind of traffic stoplight and a capsule that could make sparkling water, and she helped a tycoon build more efficient airplanes by suggesting modifications to their shape.

During the Second World War, Hedy learned that the Nazis were able to protect their submarines from torpedoes by jamming the radio signals used to control them. "I can solve that problem," she said, and she got straight to work.

With the help of a musician friend, she invented a secret communication system that could automatically change the frequency of a torpedo's radio signal, making it impossible for enemies to jam.

Her work laid the foundation for the Wi-Fi and Bluetooth technologies we all use today.

NOVEMBER 9, 1914–JANUARY 19, 2000
AUSTRIA

"TRY EVERYTHING.
JOIN EVERYTHING.
MEET EVERYBODY.
THAT'S THE SECRET OF LIFE."
– HEDY LAMARR

HORTENSIA

ORATOR

Once there was a woman who knew how to win an argument. Her name was Hortensia, and she lived through a turbulent time in the history of ancient Rome.

The Roman emperor, Julius Caesar, had recently been killed, and he was replaced as ruler by Mark Antony, Octavian, and Marcus Aemilius Lepidus. Together, they were called the triumvirs.

The triumvirs wanted to declare war on the assassins of Julius Caesar, but they needed money to pay for the conflict. So they decided to tax the property of fourteen hundred rich Roman women to finance it. Hortensia was one of them. She didn't think it made sense that women had no say in a decision that affected them, however, so she decided to do something about it.

At first, she tried to persuade the triumvirs' wives to talk to their husbands, but she wasn't successful. Flavia, Marc Antony's wife, was more interested in protecting her husband's decision than her own rights, and she threw Hortensia out of their house.

Outraged, Hortensia pushed her way into the tribunal and made her case with a memorable speech. "Why should we finance your war," she demanded, "when we have no say in the government, no honors, and no part in public office? We would gladly pay taxes to help protect our country against a foreign invasion, but you cannot force us to sponsor your civil war."

The triumvirs were furious. But Hortensia convinced so many people with her speech that the three rulers had to listen to her brilliant reasoning, and in the end, they changed their policy.

BORN 42 BCE
ITALY

"WHY SHOULD
WE PAY TAXES
WHEN WE HAVE
NO PART IN
PUBLIC OFFICE?"
– HORTENSIA

ISADORA DUNCAN

DANCER

Once upon a time, there was a girl who didn't like school. Isadora hated sitting still at a desk when she longed to leap and spin and twirl—to express all the joy of being alive through her body. Deep inside, the girl knew she was born to dance.

When she was only six years old, Isadora had already become a dance teacher. At the time, everyone thought ballet was the most beautiful type of dance in the world, but Isadora did not. She didn't like the formal elegance of classical ballet. She found it "ugly and against nature."

She said, "I want to dance like a wave on the ocean or a tree in the breeze. Natural and free."

When she was eighteen, Isadora used her last few dollars to buy a ticket on a cattle boat from America to Europe. She traveled around all the great cities—Paris, Berlin, Vienna, and London. She performed onstage and set up groundbreaking dance schools. "In my schools," she announced, "I shall not teach the children to imitate my movements, but to make their own."

While dancing, Isadora wore loose white dresses and long trailing scarves; she wanted the cloth to echo and enhance the flowing movements of her limbs. Some people thought she was indecent. "Women should not be so wild and free," they said. But Isadora didn't care! She declared herself to be a "dancer of the future ... the highest intelligence in the freest body."

C. MAY 27, 1878 – SEPTEMBER 14, 1927
UNITED STATES OF AMERICA

"YOU WERE ONCE WILD HERE.
DON'T LET THEM TAME YOU."
– ISADORA DUNCAN

J.K. ROWLING

WRITER

At six, Joanne wrote a short story about a rabbit and titled it "Rabbit." At eleven, she wrote a novel about seven cursed diamonds.

She came from a poor family, and her parents hoped she would pursue a solid career in law or economics. But she decided to study literature.

One day, she found herself completely broke. As a single mother with no job and no money, Joanne experienced the pain of failure that her parents had always warned her about. Everything she owned was in a suitcase, including the first three chapters of a story about a boy with magic powers. That boy was called Harry Potter.

Her manuscript about Harry was rejected time after time, but finally one publisher took it on. They printed just a thousand copies and asked Joanne to change her name to J.K., as they feared young boys would not want to read a book written by a woman.

Her agent told her that she shouldn't expect to make money out of her writing, but thankfully Joanne decided to keep going. The Harry Potter series went on to become the most incredible phenomenon in the history of publishing. The seven books have captured the imagination of hundreds of millions of children—and adults—all over the world, and they've redefined the meaning of children's literature.

Joanne always said failure was crucial to her success. "Had I really succeeded at anything else," she explained, "I might never have found the determination to succeed in the one arena I believed I truly belonged."

BORN JULY 31, 1965
UNITED KINGDOM

"IT IS IMPOSSIBLE TO LIVE WITHOUT
FAILING AT SOMETHING,
UNLESS YOU LIVE SO
CAUTIOUSLY THAT
YOU MIGHT AS
WELL NOT HAVE
LIVED AT ALL."
– J.K. ROWLING

ILLUSTRATION BY
PAOLA ROLLO

JEANNE BARET

HOUSEKEEPER AND EXPLORER

O nce upon a time, a housekeeper called Jeanne disguised herself as a man and sailed around the world.

Jeanne looked after the house of a French naturalist named Commerson. One day, he was invited to sail to the New World on an expedition to find and identify new species of plants. Commerson was excited, but his health was poor and he needed someone to accompany him on this long, exhausting voyage.

At the time, women weren't allowed aboard French ships, so Commerson and Jeanne came up with a plan: at the very last minute, she would get on the ship disguised as a young man called Jean, and Commerson would hire this "stranger" as his assistant. The plan worked—and the ship's captain even gave up his large cabin to the two so they would have space for all the special equipment Commerson needed.

Jeanne took good care of Commerson, but he was so ill by the time they reached South America that she took over collecting and studying the plants herself. She was unstoppable. In Rio de Janeiro, Brazil, she found a brightly colored vine that Commerson named bougainvillea after the ship's captain, Bougainville.

When Jeanne's real identity was discovered, she and Commerson decided to leave the ship and stay in Mauritius, an island off the coast of Africa. They completed two more scientific expeditions—to Madagascar and the Bourbon Islands—but then Commerson died and Jeanne was stranded. When she finally made it back to France, one year later, she had become the first woman in history to circumnavigate the globe.

JULY 27, 1740 - AUGUST 5, 1807
FRANCE

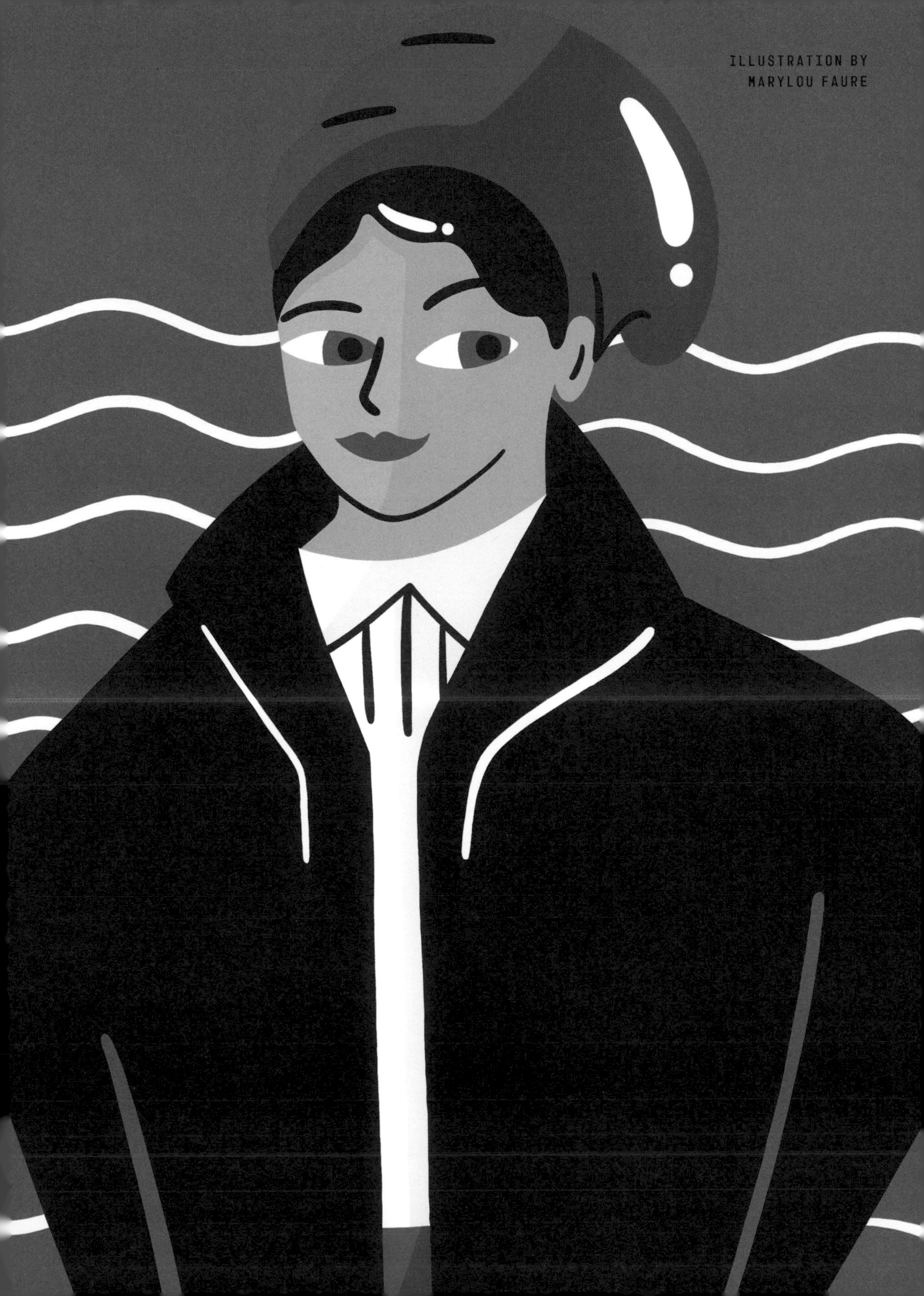

ILLUSTRATION BY
MARYLOU FAURE

JOAN BEAUCHAMP PROCTER

ZOOLOGIST

One day, a girl called Joan asked her mom and dad to get her a pet. "I don't want a puppy or a kitten," she said. "I'd love a snake! And some lizards, please." By the time she was ten, Joan was looking after lots of reptiles. One of them, a large Dalmatian wall lizard, was her favorite; they traveled everywhere together, and even sat side by side at mealtimes. When she was older, Joan took her pet crocodile to school—much to the teacher's amazement!

These creatures fascinated Joan. She became a world expert in herpetology—the branch of zoology dealing with reptiles and amphibians—and got a job at the British Natural History Museum. Then one day, London Zoo asked her to design a new reptile house. She did an excellent job and became something of a celebrity. Crowds gathered to watch her handling pythons, crocodiles, and huge Komodo dragons. She was named curator of reptiles.

A Komodo dragon named Sumbawa became Joan's special pet. Sumbawa followed her everywhere. Joan would stroke and pat her, and feed her chicken, pigeon, and eggs. Sometimes, she "steered" the dragon along by holding her tail. Joan understood these animals so well that she knew when they were sick, and exactly what to do to make them better.

Her own health problems, however, were harder to cure. She was constantly in pain, and had been for much of her life. But this didn't stop her from following her passion—even when it meant going to work in a wheelchair, with Sumbawa lumbering along happily behind her.

AUGUST 5, 1897–SEPTEMBER 20, 1931
UNITED KINGDOM

ILLUSTRATION BY
MARIJKE BUURLAGE

"WHY SHOULDN'T A WOMAN
RUN A REPTILE HOUSE?"
– JOAN BEAUCHAMP PROCTER

JOHANNA NORDBLAD

ICE DIVER

O nce upon a time, there was a free-diving champion named Johanna. She loved diving deep underwater on just a single breath, without the use of air tanks. As she swam down with nothing but the slow thump of her heartbeat in her ears, Johanna felt like she was flying.

Then one day, she had a terrible accident. Her leg was so badly broken that the doctors thought they might have to remove it. The only way to save the leg was by plunging it in ice water. It was agonizingly painful, but her leg slowly began to heal. And something else happened that no one had expected: Johanna started to enjoy the feeling of the icy coldness. "I felt it was the only place where I could get over the pain. Actually, it was very relaxing," she said.

When she was strong enough, Johanna decided to start swimming underneath ice. A film was made about one of her incredible dives. It shows a solitary figure dragging a sled to the middle of a frozen lake, leaving a trail of footprints behind her in the snow. She cuts a triangle into the ice with a saw and sits on the edge. Taking a deep breath, she slips into the black water. A different universe unfolds around her: silver and deep blue-black, silent and beautiful. She swims along like a mermaid, at peace with the world.

If it hadn't been for the accident, Johanna might never have discovered the joy of ice diving. Sometimes, she says, a curse really is a blessing in disguise.

BORN NOVEMBER 11, 1975
FINLAND

"UNDER THE ICE, THERE IS NO PLACE FOR FEAR. THERE IS
NO PLACE FOR PANIC, NO PLACE FOR MISTAKES."
– JOHANNA NORDBLAD

KATHERINE JOHNSON, DOROTHY VAUGHAN, AND MARY JACKSON

COMPUTER SCIENTISTS

Every day, Katherine, Dorothy, and Mary drove together to NASA, the agency responsible for the American space program. They were all brilliant scientists, and their job was to crack complex math problems to make sure that astronauts could travel safely to space.

When NASA bought its first IBM transistor-based computer, only a few people in the world knew how to use it for business—and no one knew how to use it for space travel! So Dorothy taught herself Fortran, the programming language the computer understood, and got the system working.

When astronaut John Glenn was about to take off for a trip orbiting the earth, he said he did not completely trust the computer and asked Katherine to check the trajectory calculations herself. "As long as she says the numbers are good ... I'm ready to go," he said.

When the opportunity to work on the **Supersonic Pressure Tunnel** came about, Mary volunteered. She specialized in the behavior of air around planes, and she became the first African American female aeronautical engineer.

Katherine, Dorothy, and Mary overcame incredible odds, but their contributions to science and technology remained unknown for many years. Today, they are celebrated as three of the most inspiring figures in the history of space travel.

KATHERINE JOHNSON, BORN AUGUST 26, 1918
DOROTHY VAUGHAN, SEPTEMBER 20, 1910-NOVEMBER 10, 2008
MARY JACKSON, APRIL 9, 1921-FEBRUARY 11, 2005
UNITED STATES OF AMERICA

"IN MATH, EITHER YOU'RE RIGHT
OR YOU'RE WRONG."
—KATHERINE JOHNSON

KATIA KRAFFT

VOLCANOLOGIST

Katia loved volcanoes. She didn't just like to look at pictures of boiling rivers of lava—she wanted to see them for real.

In college, Katia met a young man called Maurice who was as passionate about volcanoes as she was. On their first date, they realized they shared the dream of filming a volcano as it was erupting—something no one had ever done before. They fell madly in love and planned their first trip to an active volcano.

From then on, they were hooked. Whenever they heard that a volcano was about to blow, they packed their bags and rushed to the scene. To get the best shots, they would scramble up to the edge of the crater. They wore protective silver suits and helmets so they could withstand the heat from the molten lava—which was more than a thousand degrees.

Katia and Maurice's dream was to ride a boat down a lava flow! They knew their work was extremely dangerous, but they didn't care. To them, there was no sight more beautiful than a volcano erupting right before their eyes.

One day, Katia and Maurice were on the slopes of Mount Unzen, an active volcano in Japan. They were a safe distance from the summit— or so they thought. But this time, their calculations were wrong. The explosion was far larger than anyone had predicted, and it sent a boiling cloud of gases, rocks, and ash rolling down the valley. Katia, Maurice, and the members of their team had no chance to escape, and all tragically died.

APRIL 17, 1942 – JUNE 3, 1991
FRANCE

ILLUSTRATION BY
MARTINA PAUKOVA

"VOLCANOES ARE
SO POWERFUL,
SO BEAUTIFUL,
SO YOU CAN JUST
FALL IN LOVE
WITH THEM."
– KATIA KRAFFT

KHOUDIA DIOP

MODEL

Once upon a time, there was a girl whose skin was as dark as night. Her name was Khoudia, and she lived in Senegal. At school, Khoudia was bullied because of the color of her skin. Other children would call her hurtful names, and every day Khoudia would look in the mirror to see if her skin had got any lighter.

Her sister showed her the pictures of the model Alek Wek. "You're beautiful!" she assured her. "See? You could be a model too!"

One day, Khoudia and her sister were walking down a street in Milan, Italy, when they passed a giant mirror. Khoudia saw how she stood out from all the other fair-skinned people around them. "I smiled and it was like sparkles!" she said with surprise. "That's why people look at me so much—it's because I'm beautiful!"

A couple of years later, Khoudia accompanied an aunt who needed eye surgery to Paris. There, people would stop her in the streets to take pictures of her. She became a professional model and opened an Instagram account, calling herself the Melanin Goddess.

"In Senegal, a lot of girls who are as dark as me bleach their skin, because they think they aren't beautiful," she explained. "But every woman is different, and we're all beautiful in our unique way."

Today, Khoudia campaigns to prevent bullying and is very proud that her eleven-year-old brother, who is as dark as she is, told her, "I don't care what other kids say about my skin color. I love it!"

BORN DECEMBER 31, 1996
SENEGAL

"IF YOU'RE LUCKY ENOUGH
TO BE DIFFERENT,
DON'T EVER CHANGE."
— KHOUDIA DIOP

LAUREN POTTER

ACTRESS

The day she was born, Lauren was diagnosed with **Down syndrome**. Because of her condition, she couldn't walk until the age of two, but shortly after taking her first steps, she started dancing and acting classes. She loved performing, and her mom encouraged her to follow her passion from a very young age.

At school, however, her classmates were not as supportive. Bullies made fun of her—and even made her eat sand. "It was hard," Lauren remembered. "They hurt me."

As time went on, her passion for music and dance only grew stronger. She auditioned to be a cheerleader at her high school, but she didn't make the squad. A year later, though, a much bigger opportunity came her way: a chance to play a cheerleader in a national TV show called *Glee*.

Out of the thirteen girls who auditioned for the role, the one the show's producers picked was Lauren! The character she played, Becky Jackson, became so popular that kids in her former high school put posters of her on the walls. "I'm happy they can now see me as I always saw myself," Lauren said.

She enjoyed being an actress, but she also wanted to help other people with disabilities. Lauren wanted them to have the opportunity to follow their passions just as she had. She was appointed by Barack Obama to the President's Committee for People with Intellectual Disabilities, and she starred in commercials against bullying.

Today, she travels across the country giving speeches, and she says, "It feels amazing to be a role model for people with and without disabilities."

BORN MAY 10, 1990
UNITED STATES OF AMERICA

"IF YOU HAVE A DISABILITY, KEEP WORKING HARD.
WHATEVER IT TAKES, DO IT!"
– LAUREN POTTER

LEYMAH GBOWEE

PEACE ACTIVIST

Once, in Liberia, a woman stopped a war.

Her name was Leymah, and she was a single mother of four. Her country was going through a violent civil war: children were being recruited as soldiers, and hundreds of thousands of people were dying. Leymah worked hard to help those who had been traumatized by the fighting.

One day, she was invited to a conference organized by the West Africa Network for Peacebuilding. "Women like me had come from almost all eighteen countries in West Africa," Leymah recalled.

At the conference, she learned about conflict and conflict resolution. The women shared their experiences and talked about what war had taken from their lives. For Leymah, it was enlightening. "No one else," she thought, "is doing this—focusing only on women and only on building peace."

She became the leader of a program called the Women in Peacebuilding Network. To recruit other women, she went to mosques for Friday afternoon prayers, to the markets on Saturday mornings, and to churches every Sunday. All the women she spoke to were tired of a war they had never wanted in the first place—a war that was killing their children.

Leymah and the other women in her network pressured the factions at war to start peace talks. Then they gathered in front of the hotel where the negotiations were taking place to demand rapid progress. They even blocked the hotel exit to keep the negotiators from leaving until they had reached a deal.

When the Liberian civil war ended, Leymah was awarded a Nobel Peace Prize. "When women gather," she says, "great things will happen."

BORN FEBRUARY 1, 1972
LIBERIA

"WE MUST CONTINUE TO UNITE IN SISTERHOOD TO TURN
OUR TEARS INTO TRIUMPH."
– LEYMAH GBOWEE

LILIAN BLAND

AVIATOR

The first time Lilian was in a plane, it was with her boyfriend. He took her up in his glider, but when she asked, "Can I fly it?" he said no and Lilian got really mad.

Shortly after, Lilian's uncle Robert sent her a postcard of his own little plane flying over Paris. Lilian was in awe. She immediately wrote back, begging him to take her aboard as a passenger. But her uncle said no as well.

"All right, I will have to do this by myself," Lilian thought. But at the time, it wasn't easy to find a plane in Ireland. "No problem," she said to herself. "I'll build one."

Lilian read everything she could find by the Wright brothers and other famous aviators about how to build a plane. She succeeded in building a flyable biplane—an aircraft with two pairs of wings—then went on to build a full-scale glider, just like the one her boyfriend hadn't let her fly.

She called her glider the *Mayfly*—because, as she said, "It may fly, [or] it may not!"

Lilian fitted the *Mayfly* with an engine and found a nice level stretch of empty ground to use as a runway. She couldn't wait to see if her glider would get off the ground. The only problem was that the plane had no tank to hold the fuel. "Never mind," she thought. "I'll use an empty bottle instead." She did just that—and the plane soared along for about ten seconds.

The *Mayfly*—designed, built, and flown by the amazing, inventive Lilian Bland—was the first powered aircraft in Ireland.

SEPTEMBER 22, 1878 - MAY 11, 1971
UNITED KINGDOM

ILLUSTRATION BY
NOA SNIR

"I HAVE FLOWN!"
– LILIAN BLAND

LORENA OCHOA

GOLFER

Once, a girl fell out of a tree and broke both her wrists. Her arms were in casts from fingertips to shoulders for three months. When the casts came off, her bones were completely mended. "It's not a miracle," said the doctor with a smile. "I just put magic in the cast."

Lorena lived in Guadalajara, Mexico. Her house was near a country club that had a golf course. Sometimes, she would watch her dad play a round of golf on his day off.

At first, she only helped him steer his cart. But eventually, she started to play as well. It was immediately clear that, whether the doctor had something to do with it or not, Lorena had a magic touch.

At seven, she started competing in and winning golf tournaments. She also played tennis and excelled at that too! When she won the Junior World Championships in San Diego, though, she decided to focus on golf.

Lorena was tiny but strong. She became the top female golfer in the world. Her fans watched in awe when she hit drives longer than anyone else's. But her best game was with the short irons: the magic in her wrists made her unbelievably precise.

She became known as La Tigresa—the Tiger.

But Lorena wasn't happy being a world champion only in golf. She also opened a foundation that operates an innovative school called La Barranca, where 250 underprivileged kids can get a great education and spend some fun time outdoors too—playing golf, of course!

BORN NOVEMBER 15, 1981
MEXICO

ILLUSTRATION BY
CAMILLA PERKINS

"I HIT A LOT OF BAD SHOTS. YOU NEED TO
LAUGH ABOUT THEM AND KEEP MOVING."
– LORENA OCHOA

LOWRI MORGAN

ULTRAMARATHON RUNNER

Once upon a time, there was a girl called Lowri who loved to sing. She dreamt of becoming a professional singer. But life had other plans for the little girl—plans that would take her far, far away from the hills of south Wales, where she was born. Lowri became an ultramarathon runner—someone who competes in races of great distances in extreme environments.

One day, as she ran through the Amazon jungle, exhausted and dripping with sweat, she wondered what life as a singer would have been like. "A lot easier, that's for sure," she thought. She was running the Jungle Marathon—one of the toughest races on the planet. There were snakes in the trees and jaguars on the ground. She was attacked by angry hornets and had to swim across a river full of piranhas! It was terrifying, but she kept on going. She refused to give up.

From one of the hottest places in the world, Lowri then ran in one of the coldest: the Arctic. She was so cold and tired during that race that her mind started playing tricks. "I saw a park bench on the ice, and thought, 'How nice! I can sit down.' But of course it was not really there."

Just when she felt she couldn't go on, something magical happened: she heard her mother's voice. "Glory is not by never falling," her mother said, "but in the way we rise when we do fall." Lowri picked herself up and carried on, over the snow and ice, past reindeers and polar bears, until she reached the finish line in record time.

BORN 1975
UNITED KINGDOM

"I LOVE LOOKING BEHIND ME
TO THE BOTTOM OF THE MOUNTAIN AND THINKING,
'WOW, I CAN'T BELIEVE HOW FAR I'VE COME.'"
– LOWRI MORGAN

LUO DENGPING

EXTREME ROCK CLIMBER

Once upon a time, there was a girl named Luo who loved climbing. She lived in Guizhou, a spectacular place in southern China with towering rock outcrops, lush dense jungles, and terraced fields covering the hills.

The men in Luo's village had a unique tradition: they climbed up and down the terrifyingly high cliffs with no climbing gear, no safety nets, nothing but their bare hands. They gathered medicinal herbs and collected swallow droppings to use as fertilizer. They were so agile and fast that people called them the Spider-Men. Luo's father was one of them. As a little girl, Luo used to watch him climb nimbly from one ledge to the next, hundreds of feet in the air. "One day, I'll do that," she thought to herself.

When she turned fifteen, Luo started practicing on small slopes. She was the only female rock climber in Guizhou, and at first no one wanted to train her. But eventually, she convinced her father to teach her all he knew. Soon, she was climbing as high and as fast as any of the Spider-Men. She was strong, brave, and extremely good at finding cracks in the sheer rock face to grab hold of.

Today, Luo is a professional climber. Tourists love to watch her death-defying feats. Her hands are rough and calloused from hanging on to the rocks, and she loves her work. "When I get to the top, I wave the red flag," she says. "It's a fantastic feeling—like I'm on top of the world!" Everyone in her village is proud of Luo, their very own Spider-Woman.

BORN 1980
CHINA

"I WANTED TO BE A SPIDER-WOMAN.
SO I ASKED MY FATHER TO TRAIN ME FOR IT."
– LUO DENGPING

MADAME SAQUI

ACROBAT

During the French Revolution, there was a short, stocky girl who dreamt of being a tightrope walker. Marguerite's father had been an acrobat himself, but during the revolution no one had money to give to circus performers, so instead he set up a stall selling home remedies and hoped his daughter would forget her dreams.

But Marguerite was determined.

She found an old family friend from her father's circus days and begged him to train her in secret. She was brilliant! She made her debut at the age of eleven. People in the audience gasped when they saw her dance along a wire high over their heads. What incredible balance! Such grace! Such strength! Marguerite was an instant hit.

Her family formed a circus company with Marguerite as the star, and together they toured across France. When she was eighteen, she met a great acrobat called Julian Saqui. They fell in love and were married, and she chose to become Madame Saqui.

Madame Saqui knew she was destined for greatness. At the height of her career, she performed at the world-famous Tivoli Gardens in Paris, walking up a steep rope with fireworks exploding all around her. Even Napoleon, the emperor of France, was captivated by her, and she devised a show to commemorate his victory in battle.

Her most daring feat was to walk on a rope stretched between the towers of Notre-Dame Cathedral, hundreds of feet in the air. She became a bright star shining in the sky of Paris, and her performances are still remembered today as extraordinary displays of courage and talent.

FEBRUARY 26, 1786 – JANUARY 21, 1866
FRANCE

ILLUSTRATION BY
LAURA JUNGER

MADONNA

SINGER, SONGWRITER, AND BUSINESSWOMAN

Once, in a small town split in half by a river, a star was born. Her name was Madonna. She was smart and got top grades in school. But she always realized that she was a little bit different. More than anything, Madonna knew exactly what she wanted and would not let anyone change her dreams. Some people felt intimidated by her strength and clarity of mind, but Madonna didn't let them hold her back.

When she was twenty years old, she moved to New York City with just thirty-five dollars in her pocket. It was the first time she had taken a plane—the first time she had taken a cab! "It was the bravest thing I've ever done," she later said.

Madonna worked as a singer in clubs and as a waitress in coffee shops. She worked hard. She tried and failed and tried again, numerous times.

In those days, it was very rare for female artists to be the masters of their own destiny: they would let their male managers, producers, and agents make most of their decisions for them. Not Madonna. "I am my own experiment," she declared. "I am my own work of art."

Through her music, Madonna inspired hundreds of millions of people to stay true to themselves and stand proud, even in the face of adversity. "I've been popular and unpopular, successful and unsuccessful, loved and loathed, and I know how meaningless it all is. Therefore I feel free to take whatever risks I want," she explained.

Her huge talent, tremendous self-discipline, and fierce determination have made her one of the most influential pop artists in history.

BORN AUGUST 16, 1958
UNITED STATES OF AMERICA

"I HAVE THE SAME GOAL I'VE HAD
EVER SINCE I WAS A GIRL:
I WANT TO RULE THE WORLD."
— MADONNA

MARIE THARP

GEOLOGIST

Marie wanted to study the earth's crust, so she completed a master's degree in geology at the University of Michigan.

Today we know that millions of years ago, almost all the earth's land was united in a supercontinent called Pangea and surrounded by a superocean called Panthalassa. In Marie's time, though, this was still just a theory based on the simple observation that the coastlines of South America and Africa looked like matching pieces of a gigantic jigsaw puzzle. In between the continents there were now huge oceans. To prove that such distant lands had once been united, the ocean floor had to be mapped.

People assumed that the bottom of the ocean was flat, and this idea wasn't challenged until geologists started to use sonar onboard ships. The sonar bounced sound waves off the bottom of the ocean, and it was Marie's job to make sense of the readings. She crunched numbers, took measurements by hand, and became the first person ever to piece together a map of the North Atlantic seafloor with its mountains and valleys. "The whole world was spread out before me," she recalled.

Marie discovered that at the bottom of the Atlantic Ocean, there was an incredibly deep rift valley that looked just like the Great Rift Valley in Africa. It formed part of a system that encircled the entire globe!

She showed that the ocean floor was spreading apart, which meant that the continents were drifting away from each other. This in turn proved that they had indeed been united millions of years ago, when the earth was young.

JULY 30, 1920–AUGUST 23, 2006
UNITED STATES OF AMERICA

ILLUSTRATION BY
BARBARA DZIADOSZ

"I HAD A
FASCINATING JIGSAW PUZZLE
TO PIECE TOGETHER"
— MARIE THARP

MARINA ABRAMOVIĆ

PERFORMANCE ARTIST

Once upon a time, a woman in a long red dress sat silently at a wooden table. Her name was Marina, and she was a world-famous artist.

She was sitting in a plain white room inside the Museum of Modern Art in New York City. Marina had decided she would sit there seven hours a day for a hundred days. On the other side of the table was an empty chair. Anyone who wanted to could sit across from her. As long as they kept silent and looked her in the eye, they could sit there as long as they liked.

Marina's idea was simple yet groundbreaking. Thousands lined up for hours to sit with her and be in her presence—or even just to see her and another stranger staring at each other.

Many people were moved to tears by Marina's performance. It's not often we take the time to simply sit and look at each other, without saying anything. It's not often we feel truly "seen" by another person.

A record-breaking half a million people visited the show. For forty years, Marina had been an artist. Not all her performances were as successful as *The Artist Is Present*, but she never stopped experimenting—she never let fear get in her way. "If you experiment, you have to fail," she explained. "By definition, experimenting means going to territory where you've never been, where failure is very possible. How can you know you're going to succeed? Having the courage to face the unknown is so important."

BORN NOVEMBER 30, 1946
SERBIA

"THE HARDEST THING TO DO
IS SOMETHING THAT IS
CLOSE TO NOTHING."
- MARINA ABRAMOVIĆ

MARTA VIEIRA DA SILVA

SOCCER PLAYER

Marta loved to play soccer, and she was always the first to be picked by the boys when teams were made. Her mom couldn't afford to send her to school, so Marta used to sell fruit in the public market to help her family get by. In her spare time, she played soccer in the streets.

One day, when Marta was fourteen, a famous soccer coach saw her playing with a group of boys. Her speed, superb control, and strong left foot amazed the coach. She knew that Marta would become a champion, and she helped her join the Vasco da Gama football club.

Despite her talent, Marta didn't have an easy career. In Brazil, soccer is still considered a man's game, and there isn't much funding for women's teams. When she was seventeen, Marta decided to accept an offer to move to Sweden. There, she won several league titles and a record five consecutive World Player of the Year Awards from FIFA, soccer's international governing body.

Her fancy footwork and blistering goals earned her the nickname Pelé con Faldas (Pelé with Skirts), after the greatest soccer player of all time, but she didn't pay too much attention to that. She captained the Brazilian national team in her trademark number 10 yellow jersey, leading it to two silver medals at the Olympic Games.

Marta was appointed a United Nations Goodwill Ambassador for her role in promoting equality in sport. "I feel proud," she said, "when I know that little girls and boys look up to me as an example."

BORN FEBRUARY 19, 1986
BRAZIL

"I WAS CALLED A 'MACHO WOMAN.' IT MOTIVATED ME."
– MARTA VIEIRA DA SILVA

MARY FIELDS

MAIL CARRIER

Mary was an incredibly strong woman.

When a friend who was a nun fell sick, she rushed to the convent to look after her. Mother Amadeus recovered, but Mary stayed on to help out. She took care of four hundred chickens and drove a stagecoach to transport visitors to and from the convent.

One night, wolves attacked the stagecoach. Mary fought them off all night long, and in the morning she made it back to the convent safe and sound.

Stagecoach Mary, as she was called, spent ten years working there, but when a man complained that she was making two dollars more than he was each month, she got angry and grabbed her gun. There was a shoot-out: six guns were emptied in the back of the nunnery, and the man was injured. The bishop fired Mary and gave the man a raise.

Mary opened a restaurant, but because she gave food to everyone, whether they could pay for it or not, she went out of business in just a few months. At sixty, she applied to be a mail carrier. She got the job because she was the fastest person to hitch up a team of six horses. She was the second woman and the first African American woman to work for the United States Postal Service.

Mary never missed a day on the job. Come hell or high water, she was on her stagecoach delivering mail to the most remote homesteads in Montana. In her spare time, she babysat children, spending all the money she made to buy them presents.

1832-1914
UNITED STATES OF AMERICA

"I CAN KNOCK OUT ANY COWBOY IN CASCADE
WITH A SINGLE PUNCH."
– MARY FIELDS

MARY KINGSLEY

EXPLORER

Once upon a time, there was a girl named Mary whose brother was sent to school. She wasn't, because her family wanted her to take care of the house. The only thing Mary was taught was German: her father wanted her to translate some scientific books for him. She spent countless hours in his library. The books about voyages to faraway lands were her favorites.

When her parents died, Mary finally had time to do what she wanted with her life. She decided to travel to the most magical and unknown place she could think of: West Africa. Her friends and family all advised her against it. "It's dangerous," they said. "A woman can't travel all that way alone. And why on earth do you want to go to Africa?"

Mary didn't listen to them and went anyway. She traveled from village to village throughout West Africa. She canoed up the Ogowe River, and she was the first woman to climb Mount Cameroon. Being a white woman (and sometimes the first white person the local people had ever seen), she knew she was an oddity. Mary wanted to be a part of the community, not just a scientific observer, so she started trading cloth for rubber. She recorded information about the geography of West Africa, and she collected samples of **flora and fauna** from an area that was almost unknown to Europeans at the time.

She led a life of adventure, explored the complexity of African cultures, and challenged many racist stereotypes spread by other explorers.

NOVEMBER 13, 1862 – JUNE 3, 1900
UNITED KINGDOM

"THE GRIM, GRAND AFRICAN FORESTS ARE LIKE A GREAT LIBRARY. I AM NOW BUSILY LEARNING THE ALPHABET OF THEIR LANGUAGE."
— MARY KINGSLEY

MARY SEACOLE

NURSE

O nce there was a little girl named Mary who was great at curing her dolls. If one had a fever, Mary would lay a wet facecloth on her forehead. If another's tummy hurt, she'd give her pretend hot tea.

Mary's mother had learned the ancient African art of using herbs to make medicines, and she cured lots of illnesses in Kingston, Jamaica, the town where they lived. By the time she was twelve, Mary was already helping her cure real people!

When she grew up, Mary started to travel, which was very unusual for a woman at the time. She went to the Bahamas, Haiti, and Cuba to find out how the people there used herbs to treat the sick. In Panama, she risked her life to help local nurses and doctors cure patients during a cholera epidemic.

When the Crimean War broke out, Mary traveled to London to ask if the British Army needed help on the battlefront. The army said no because they were suspicious of women practicing medicine, so Mary went to Crimea on her own and opened the British Hotel, a place where wounded soldiers could recover their strength before making the long journey home.

Mary traveled right to the front lines with two mules to bring medicines and food to soldiers. For her, any wounded soldier was a wounded human being: she didn't look at uniforms and treated men from both sides, often while bullets were flying and cannons thundered all around.

When she went back home, Mary wrote a best-selling book called *Wonderful Adventures of Mrs. Seacole in Many Lands*.

NOVEMBER 23, 1805 – MAY 14, 1881
JAMAICA

"THE GRATEFUL WORDS
AND SMILE
WHICH REWARDED ME
FOR BINDING UP A WOUND
OR GIVING A COOLING DRINK
WAS A PLEASURE WORTH
RISKING LIFE FOR
AT ANY TIME."
— MARY SEACOLE

MARY SHELLEY

WRITER

Once upon a time, there was a girl named Mary whose mother died when she was just a baby. Her stepmother wasn't kind to her, and Mary missed having a mom tremendously. But she found comfort in the huge library they had at home. Every day, Mary would borrow a different book and go to her mother's grave to read it.

The books carried her away, far from the house where she felt lonely and unhappy. Soon enough, Mary started to write her own stories and poems.

One day, she met a young poet called Percy. They had their first date by Mary's mom's grave and fell deeply in love. They ran away to Paris to be together.

As they traveled across Europe, they became friends with many other artists and writers. One stormy night, Mary, Percy, and a few friends started telling one another scary stories. After a while, one of their friends proposed that they all go back to their rooms and write ghost stories, and then see whose story was the most frightening.

That night, Mary came up with the idea of a mad scientist who builds a monster from bits of dead bodies and brings it to life using electricity. Everyone agreed: Mary's story of Dr. Victor Frankenstein was the scariest of them all.

Her novel became an incredible success, and even after two hundred years, people still love to read about Doctor Frankenstein and the terrible monster he created—all dreamt up by the amazingly imaginative Mary Shelley.

AUGUST 30, 1797–FEBRUARY 1, 1851
UNITED KINGDOM

"BEWARE; FOR I AM FEARLESS,
AND THEREFORE POWERFUL."
– MARY SHELLEY

MARYAM MIRZAKHANI

MATHEMATICIAN

Maryam was never interested in math until the day her brother told her about a cool problem: "How do you add together all the numbers from 1 to 100?"

He explained that there were two ways to get the answer: a long and boring one, and a short and beautiful one that a mathematician called Carl Friedrich Gauss had discovered when he was still in elementary school.

Gauss took all the numbers and added them together in pairs—the first and the last, the second and the second to last, and so on. He noticed that 1 + 100 = 101, 2 + 99 = 101, 3 + 98 = 101, etc., so he was able to conclude that the total would be fifty lots of 101, which is 5050. Easy!

Maryam was hooked.

In high school, she competed in the International Mathematical Olympiad, winning a gold medal in two consecutive years. She became interested in the geometry of complex surfaces. "Everyone knows that the shortest path between two points on a flat surface is a straight line, but what about when the surface is curved, like in a doughnut or a teapot?" she asked. Maryam found joy in discovering simple, elegant solutions to these complicated problems. "The more time I spend doing mathematics, the more excited I get!"

One day, her phone rang. "You've won the Fields Medal," said a voice on the other end of the line. Maryam hung up, thinking it was a joke. But it wasn't! She was the first Iranian—and the first woman in history—to win the world's most prestigious award for mathematics.

MAY 3, 1977 – JULY 14, 2017
IRAN

"THE BEAUTY OF MATHEMATICS
ONLY SHOWS ITSELF TO
MORE PATIENT FOLLOWERS."
— MARYAM MIRZAKHANI

MATA HARI

SPY

Once upon a time, a young woman named Margaretha saw an advertisement in a newspaper. It said, "Wanted: bride." She answered the ad, married a military captain based in the Dutch East Indies, and moved to Indonesia. There, she studied the local traditions and joined a dance company.

But her marriage was unhappy, and when it ended, Margaretha moved to Paris. At that time, anything from "the exotic east" was very fashionable, so she pretended to be a Hindu temple dancer. She draped herself in veils and even gave herself a stage name: Mata Hari, meaning "eye of the day" in the Malay language.

She danced with the grace of a wild animal. She wore skimpy costumes, a bra studded with jewels, and skin-colored body stockings. She became an instant hit!

When Mata Hari was forty, she fell in love with a young Russian army captain who had lost an eye on a First World War battlefield. To support him, she needed a new job, so she became a spy for France.

She traveled across Europe by train and by boat. She dyed and changed her hairstyle many times, and became a master of disguise. She found out about German submarines along the coast of Morocco and sent the information back to France in letters written with invisible ink.

But the French wrongly suspected that she was also spying for the Germans, and they arrested her as a double agent. She was sentenced to death. As she stood before the firing squad, she blew the soldiers a kiss. Mata Hari died as she had lived: fearless and free.

AUGUST 7, 1876 – OCTOBER 15, 1917
THE NETHERLANDS

"I WAS NOT CONTENT
AT HOME, I WANTED TO
LIVE LIKE A COLORFUL
BUTTERFLY IN THE SUN."
– MATA HARI

MATILDA OF CANOSSA

FEUDAL RULER

Long ago, in an ancient time of kings, popes, and castles, there was a woman so powerful that everyone wanted to become her friend. Her name was Matilda.

Matilda ruled over a huge realm that spanned black forests and green lakes, white mountains and golden shores. She lived in Italy in a time called the Middle Ages, when the two biggest powers were the Roman Catholic Church and the Holy Roman Empire. The head of the Holy Roman Empire was Henry IV, Matilda's cousin. The head of the Catholic Church was Pope Gregory VII, Matilda's friend.

One day, Henry realized that Gregory was becoming too powerful. So he declared that the people of the Holy Roman Empire no longer had to be loyal to the pope. Gregory was furious and gathered a huge army to fight back.

Henry asked Matilda for help. She had a powerful army of her own, and she could have backed her cousin in his campaign. But Matilda refused. "I will only help you obtain the pope's forgiveness," she said.

She arranged a meeting between the two men at her magnificent castle in Canossa, in northern Italy. It was winter, and the forest surrounding her castle was covered in snow.

Henry spent three days and three nights kneeling barefoot in the snow, to show repentance. When he was finally allowed to enter the castle, the pope forgave him. But their truce didn't last long.

The battle between the Holy Roman Empire and the Catholic Church had just begun, and Matilda had to lead many military expeditions against the emperor's army to protect the pope. After twenty years of battles, she was crowned imperial vicar and vice-queen of Italy.

MARCH 1046 – JULY 24, 1115
ITALY

ILLUSTRATION BY
ELISABETTA STOINICH

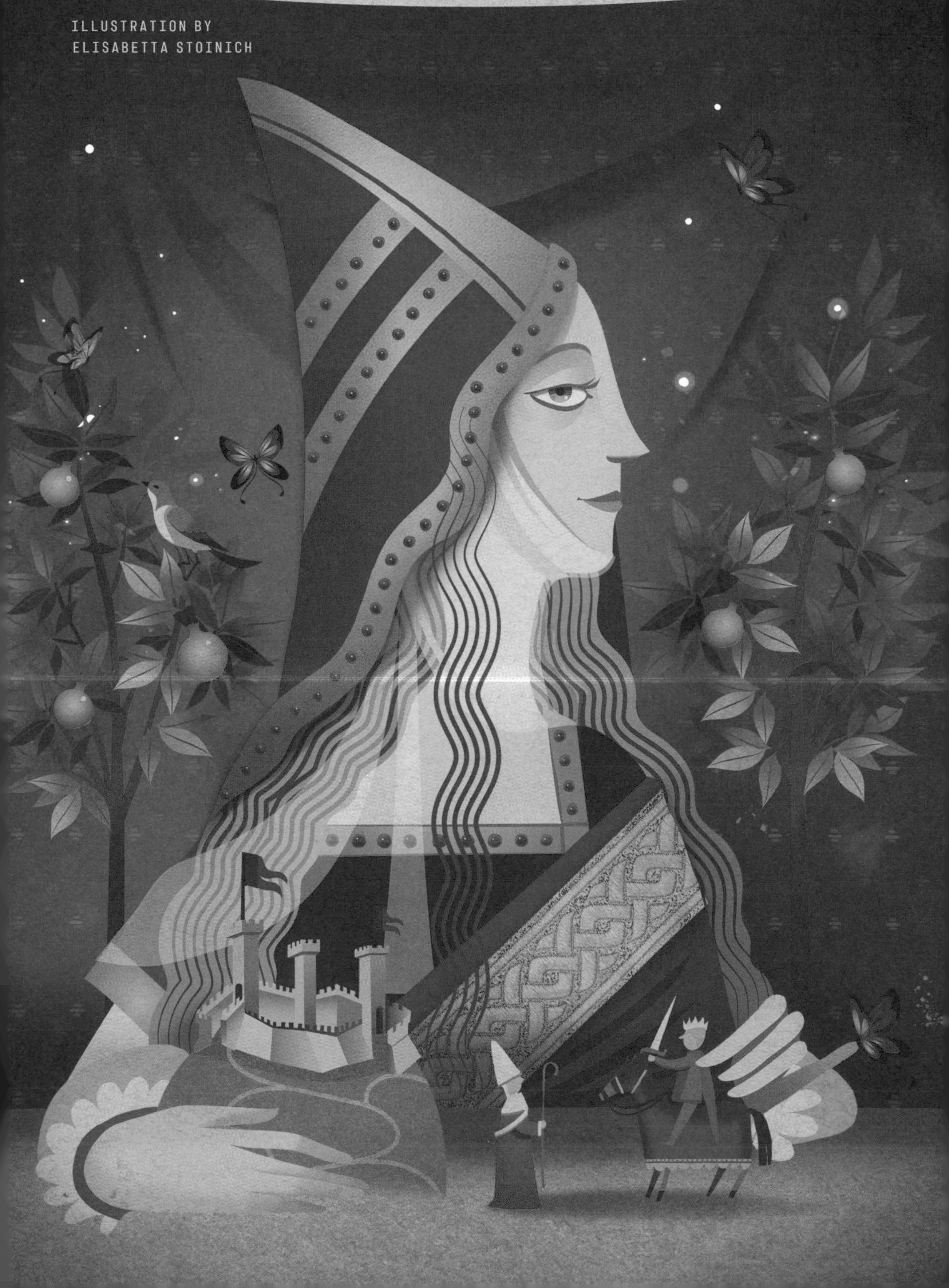

MERRITT MOORE

QUANTUM PHYSICIST AND BALLERINA

O nce upon a time, there was a girl who loved science and ballet. She was equally talented at both, but everyone said: "You'll have to choose. Science or art? Physics or ballet?"

Merritt tried to give up ballet many times. She even burned her pointe shoes! But she always started dancing again. Eventually, she joined the Zurich Ballet Company and became a professional ballerina. At the same time, she was also researching physics at Harvard University. One minute she would be in her tutu and pointe shoes, and the next she'd be in a lab coat.

It was hard. "Sometimes I felt overwhelmed," she said. "I would be in the lab for twenty hours a day, even sleeping there. But I knew I had to dance." She would take a break from work, sneak out to a stairwell, and practice ballet there. When she did, she found that she came back to the lab with a fresh perspective. And she discovered that physics helped her understand dance too. "I think it's so important for scientists to explore art. You have to think about concepts with imagination and creativity."

The two parts of her life came together beautifully in a dance piece called *Zero Point*, which explored a concept from **quantum physics** called zero-point energy.

Today, Merritt is finishing her PhD at Oxford University, and she still keeps dancing. Her favorite quote is from one of the greatest scientists in history, Albert Einstein: "Life is like riding a bicycle. To keep your balance, you must keep moving." And that's just what Merritt intends to do!

BORN FEBRUARY 24, 1988
CHINA

"I WANT TO SHATTER ALL THE STEREOTYPES.
THE DREAM IS TO CONTINUE COMBINING
PHYSICS AND DANCE."
– MERRITT MOORE

MOLLY KELLY,
DAISY KADIBILL, AND GRACIE FIELDS

FREEDOM FIGHTERS

One day, a white man in a car chased three Aboriginal girls and a woman through the Australian desert. The woman screamed and kicked and tried to protect Molly, Daisy, and Gracie, but the man caught hold of the girls and drove away, disappearing in a cloud of dark orange sand.

At the time, white settlers in Australia used to abduct children who had both white and Aboriginal parents so they could detain them in camps and train them to work as servants for white families. The man took the three girls to one of those camps.

Molly was fourteen when she decided to flee from the camp with her sister, Daisy, and their cousin, Gracie. "Look," she said to the two younger girls, pointing at a dark cloud on the horizon, "it's about to rain. Now's our chance to run. The rain will wash away our tracks!"

As they walked, Molly, Daisy, and Gracie hunted for food, waded across rivers, slept under bushes, and took turns carrying each other. They knew there was a rabbit-proof fence that ran across Australia from north to south. So they followed it north to find their village. They walked for nine weeks. Finally, they made it!

Years later, Molly's daughter wrote a book called *Follow the Rabbit-Proof Fence*, which inspired a movie about Molly, Daisy, and Gracie's incredible story.

MOLLY KELLY C. 1917–JANUARY 13, 2004
DAISY KADIBILL BORN C. 1923
GRACIE FIELDS BORN 1920
AUSTRALIA

ILLUSTRATION BY
SARA OLMOS

"WE ARE DESERT PEOPLE,
AND WE WILL SURVIVE."
– MOLLY KELLY

NADIA COMANECI

GYMNAST

When she was six years old, Nadia wanted to do only one thing: cart-wheels. At the time, cartwheels were a very big deal in her country, Romania, but Nadia didn't know that yet.

One day, she was playing in the schoolyard when she was spotted by a famous gymnastics coach named Béla Károlyi. He thought that with the right training, Nadia could become a great gymnast and bring glory to the Communist regime in Romania.

Training was hard. If the kids made a mistake, Béla would beat them with his huge hands. They had to train for six hours a day, seven days a week. He wanted his gymnasts to be perfect.

And Nadia became perfect—literally. At the age of fourteen, she scored a 10 at the Olympic Games in Montreal. No gymnast had ever received a perfect score before. People were amazed at her faultless performances on the beam, the vault, the uneven bars—Nadia became a legend.

In fact, she became so famous that the Romanian leader grew worried she would overshadow him. He wouldn't let her leave the country for any reason other than to compete.

So Nadia decided to escape. One morning, she walked for six hours through muddy woodlands and crossed the border into Hungary on foot. From there, she moved to the United States, where she was welcomed as a refugee.

In America, Nadia started a family and built a business. She loved gym-nastics and worked to promote it the way she liked the most: as a free woman.

BORN NOVEMBER 12, 1961
ROMANIA

"YOU MUST FIGURE OUT YOUR OWN DESTINATION AND THE BEST ROUTE TO GET THERE BECAUSE NO ONE ELSE KNOWS THE WAY."
– NADIA COMANECI

NADIA MURAD

HUMAN RIGHTS ACTIVIST

In the village of Kocho, there was a girl named Nadia who dreamt of becoming a history teacher or a makeup artist. Nadia belonged to the Yazidi religion, an ancient faith indigenous to northern Iraq.

One terrible day when Nadia was nineteen, a terrorist group called ISIS invaded Kocho, killed her brothers, and kidnapped her and many other Yazidi women.

Nadia was held hostage by men who hurt her badly. She was desperate, but she constantly looked for opportunities to escape. One day, she noticed that her captors had forgotten to lock the door. Without a moment's hesitation, she slipped out and ran!

A neighboring family helped her leave the region and reach a refugee camp, where she would be safe. "I might not be a history teacher or a makeup artist," she thought, "but I'll do all I can to help other women who are still prisoners of ISIS."

Nadia was resettled in Germany, where she started working with a non-profit organization.

It was hard for her to talk about what she'd been through. When something really painful happens, we wish all the memories would go away. But Nadia realized that if she kept silent, no one would know what was happening to girls like her, so she found the courage to speak out.

She told her story to journalists and spoke before the United Nations. Thanks to her testimony, global leaders learned about the terrible violence being perpetrated by ISIS fighters.

Nadia was nominated for a Nobel Peace Prize.

BORN 1993
IRAQ

"I WILL GO BACK TO MY LIFE WHEN WOMEN IN CAPTIVITY GO BACK TO THEIR LIVES, WHEN MY COMMUNITY HAS A PLACE, WHEN I SEE PEOPLE ACCOUNTABLE FOR THEIR CRIMES."
– NADIA MURAD

NADINE GORDIMER

WRITER AND ACTIVIST

Once upon a time in South Africa, there was a girl who cared deeply about justice and equality. Her name was Nadine. Back then, South Africa was still under a brutal system called apartheid, which segregated and discriminated against black people. Nadine was white and could see what a difference this single fact made to her life. She could go to any school, but her black friends couldn't. She could go to movie theaters, but her black friends couldn't. She could enter any shops she liked, but her black friends couldn't.

When the police opened fire on a crowd of protesters, killing sixty-nine people, Nadine decided to join the anti-apartheid movement. She wanted to tell the world the truth about what was happening in South Africa.

One day, she met a brilliant man called Nelson Mandela—a lawyer who would later become the country's first black president. Mandela was determined to end apartheid through peaceful political means, and he and Nadine immediately became friends. When Mandela was arrested and tried for his political activism, Nadine helped him edit a famous speech he gave in his own defense, called "I Am Prepared to Die."

The South African government banned several of Nadine's works for years, but she continued to write relentlessly: the whole world had discovered her voice and wanted to listen to her epic message of freedom and justice. She received a Nobel Prize for Literature and lived long enough to see the apartheid era come to an end.

NOVEMBER 20, 1923 – JULY 13, 2014
SOUTH AFRICA

"THE TRUTH
ISN'T ALWAYS BEAUTY,
BUT THE HUNGER
FOR IT IS."
– NADINE GORDIMER

NEFERTITI

QUEEN

Long ago in ancient Egypt, there ruled a mysterious queen called Nefertiti. Her name meant "a beautiful woman has come," but it offered no clue as to where she had come from. Nefertiti was as **enigmatic** as she was powerful.

She had six daughters and reigned alongside her husband, Akhenaten. The two wore the same crown and fought side by side in battles. Nefertiti promoted a radically new art style, and she changed Egypt from a polytheistic society, or one that believed in many gods, into a culture that worshipped only one: Aten, the sun god.

Then one day, Nefertiti disappeared.

Even now, no one knows what happened to her. If she had died, she would have received a royal burial like other kings and queens, but her tomb has never been found. Some believe that she outlived her husband, because images of her stood at each corner of his tomb. Some believe that when her husband died, she began to dress as a man and changed her name to Pharaoh Smenkhkare to become Egypt's sole ruler.

A few years ago, archaeologists were working in the tomb of another great king, Tutankhamun. One of them noticed some strange cracks in a wall. Could there be another burial chamber hidden behind it? Using a special underground radar, the archaeologists discovered that there was, in fact, a room there!

Was it the tomb of ancient Egypt's long-lost queen? Nobody knows—yet. Until they can open the chamber without damaging the fragile walls, Nefertiti's fate still lies wrapped in mystery.

C. 1370 BCE - C. 1330 BCE
EGYPT

ILLUSTRATION BY
ELENI KALORKOTI

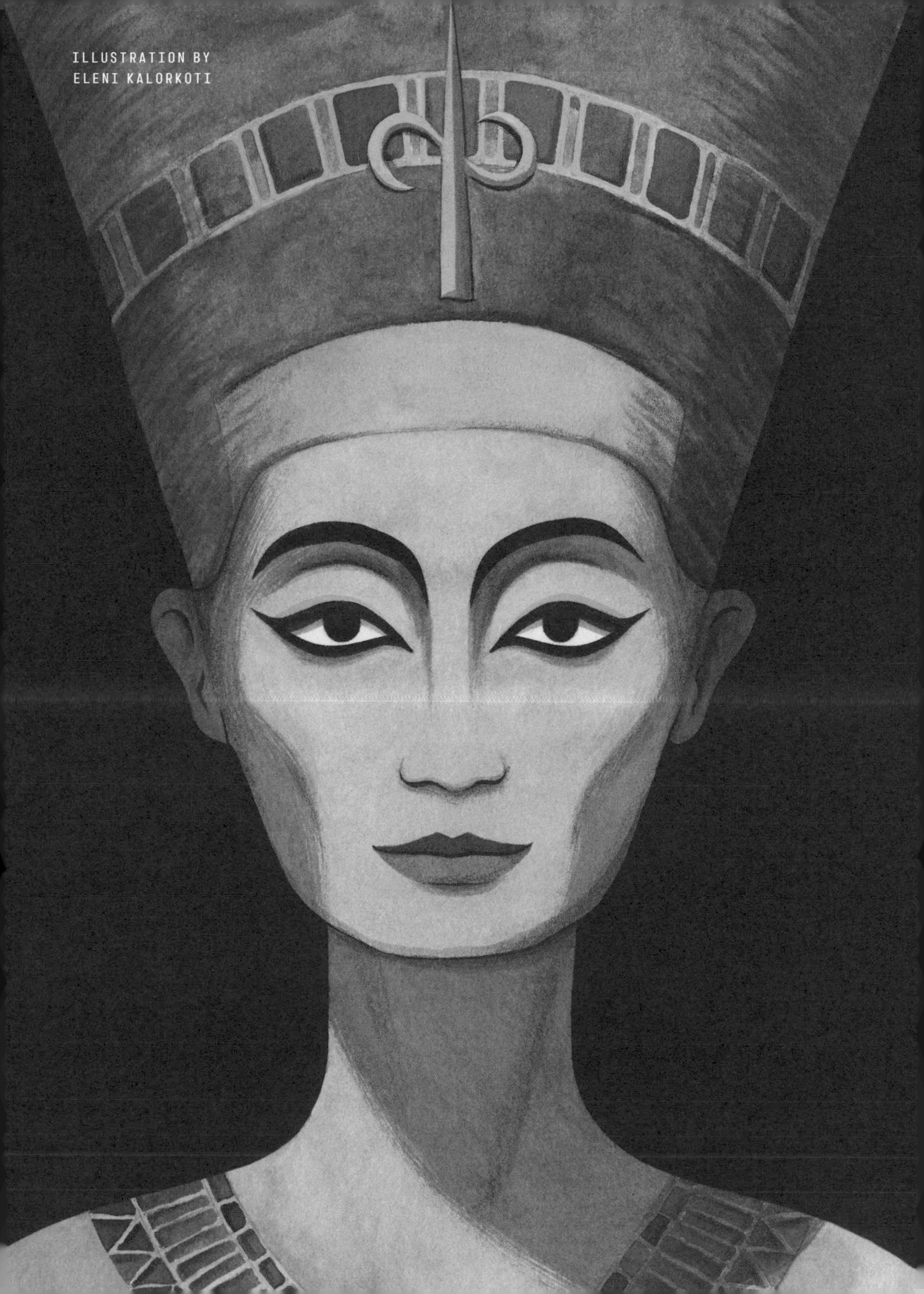

OPRAH WINFREY

TV HOST, ACTRESS, AND BUSINESSWOMAN

Once there was a little girl who interviewed crows. She also interviewed her corncob dolls, and she was so good at reciting from the Bible that people nicknamed her the Preacher.

Her name was Oprah and she loved to talk, but her family didn't listen. Her mother brushed her away, saying, "Be quiet! I don't have time for you." Her grandmother never let her cry, even when she beat the girl. "People will think you're weak," she said.

But keeping everything bottled up inside was unbearable.

So Oprah kept looking for opportunities to speak out. She kept looking for people who would listen to what she had to say. First, she joined the public speaking team in high school, then she took a job at a local radio station, and eventually she joined a Baltimore TV news show as a co-anchor.

Her family and friends were excited. But deep inside, Oprah wasn't sure that reporting the news was what she loved the most. She was fired from the show and given a low-rated early morning talk show. Oprah thought her career was over. Instead, while interviewing an ice cream seller, she discovered her greatest talent. People started to love the show because she really listened to her guests. If they cried, she felt their sadness. If they were angry, she understood their pain. And if they were happy, she laughed with them.

Oprah became the queen of talk shows. She moved on to national television, launched her own network, and became a multi-billionaire and one of the most generous philanthropists in history.

BORN JANUARY 29, 1954
UNITED STATES OF AMERICA

"YOU GET IN LIFE
WHAT YOU HAVE
THE COURAGE
TO ASK FOR."
– OPRAH WINFREY

PAULINE LÉON

REVOLUTIONARY

P auline was born in a chocolate shop in Paris. Her parents, like most people in France at that time, were simple, hardworking folk. They were part of what was known as the Third Estate—people who were neither rich landowners nor priests in the Catholic Church.

The people of the Third Estate worked hard every day, but for most, there was never enough food on the table. The rich didn't pay as much in taxes—a situation that people like Pauline thought was unfair. She wanted freedom and equality for everyone—and she wanted it now.

At the age of twenty-one, Pauline helped to start a revolution. At the time, women were not supposed to get involved in politics, but Pauline didn't care: she wanted to fight for her country. She believed that it was a citizen's duty to protect her nation, regardless of her class or gender.

One morning, about a thousand people decided to storm a Parisian fortress called the Bastille. Pauline was among them, armed with a pike. It was the beginning of the mother of all revolutions, the French Revolution—an event that would shape the future of Europe for centuries to come.

Pauline encouraged other women to take part in the revolution, and she founded a group called *femmes sans culottes*, or "women without breeches." Breeches were fancy silk pants worn by the nobility. Revolutionary women wore sturdy trousers instead.

Eventually, the French Revolution overthrew the monarchy, established a republic, and altered the course of history. And it's all thanks to citizens such as Pauline Léon, the revolutionary born in a chocolate shop.

SEPTEMBER 28, 1768 – OCTOBER 5, 1838

FRANCE

"LIBERTY,
EQUALITY,
FRATERNITY!"
—MOTTO OF THE
FRENCH REVOLUTION

PEGGY GUGGENHEIM

ART COLLECTOR

Once upon a time, there was a girl who inherited a fortune. Her name was Peggy, and her dad had died tragically when the *Titanic* sank. She was just fourteen years old.

Peggy loved to travel, but even more than that, she loved art and artists. To meet as many artists as she could, she worked as a clerk in an avant-garde bookstore in Manhattan, and later she moved to Paris, where she became friends with some of the world's most talented writers and painters.

Peggy was on a mission to build a collection of the finest works of modern art in the world. She chose carefully, buying one painting a day with a very clear idea of who should be included in her collection.

During the Second World War, Peggy was terrified that her priceless paintings would be destroyed by the bombs falling on Paris. She asked curators at the Louvre Museum for help, but they told her she didn't have anything worth protecting. Braque, Picasso, Klee, Dali, Magritte—not worth protecting? Peggy was outraged. She ended up storing her paintings in a friend's barn outside Paris.

After the war, Peggy moved to Venice, Italy. She floated around the city in her private gondola with her beloved dogs on her lap, always sporting a pair of jazzy sunglasses.

She was a driving force in the male-dominated art world of the twentieth century. The Peggy Guggenheim Collection—one of the most important museums in Italy—is located in her former Venetian home, right on the banks of the Grand Canal.

AUGUST 26, 1898–DECEMBER 23, 1979
UNITED STATES OF AMERICA

"I LOOK BACK ON MY LIFE WITH GREAT JOY. I ALWAYS DID WHAT I WANTED AND NEVER CARED WHAT ANYONE THOUGHT."
– PEGGY GUGGENHEIM

POORNA MALAVATH

MOUNTAINEER

Once upon a time, a girl called Poorna went on a rock-climbing expedition with her classmates. When they arrived at Bhongir Rock, in southern India, she looked up at the huge cliff that she was supposed to climb. Her legs shook and there were tears in her eyes. "I'll never make it," she thought.

But Poorna's teacher, a local police officer, encouraged her. "You can do it," he said. So she tried. When she reached the top, she shouted for joy. "I'm not afraid of anything now," she said. "I can conquer Mount Everest!" And she wasn't just saying it—Poorna actually wanted to climb the highest mountain in the world.

Before setting off for that next adventure, she had to train hard. She built up her stamina playing kabbadi—a sport similar to a high-energy version of tag. She traveled to the high plateaus of northern India in the freezing winter, and she climbed to the top of Mount Renock, one of the most challenging peaks in the Himalayas.

When she was ready, she joined an expedition to scale Mount Everest. She wasn't at all afraid when she first saw the mighty mountain. "It's not that tall," she said to her coach. "We can do that in a day."

Well, it took fifty-two days to get to the top, but when she reached the summit, Poorna, age thirteen, became the youngest girl ever to make it.

Poorna went on to climb to the top of Mount Kilimanjaro, in Tanzania, but her highest aspiration is to become a police officer—just like the teacher who helped her conquer her fear.

BORN APRIL 2000
INDIA

ILLUSTRATION BY
PRIYA KURIYAN

"I WANTED TO PROVE THAT GIRLS CAN DO ANYTHING."
– POORNA MALAVATH

QIU JIN

REVOLUTIONARY

Once, a girl named Qiu Jin followed her father's orders and married a wealthy merchant whom she didn't love. Unsurprisingly, theirs was not a happy marriage.

"That man is worse than an animal ... He treats me as less than nothing," Qiu Jin wrote. She dreamt of becoming a famous poet, but her husband made fun of her and told her she'd never reach her goals.

At that time, China was evolving from an empire ruled by a dynasty into a republic run by the people. Every day, revolutionary groups were formed and underground newspapers spread new ideas about the future of the country. Qiu Jin wanted to be part of this transformation, so she left her abusive husband and moved to Japan.

There, she educated herself about women's rights, and she learned that the ancient practice of **foot-binding** was hurting millions of Chinese girls.

When she returned home, Qiu Jin founded the *Chinese Women's Journal*. She also began encouraging women to overthrow the Qing dynasty. "With all my heart," she wrote, "I beseech and beg my two hundred million countrywomen to assume their responsibility as citizens. Arise! Arise! Chinese women, arise!"

Qiu Jin opened a school that was supposed to train sports teachers but actually trained revolutionaries. She was warned that government officials were on their way to arrest her, yet she refused to run away. "I'm willing to die for the cause," she said.

She was executed, but she became a national hero and a symbol of women's independence in China and all over the world.

NOVEMBER 8, 1875 – JULY 15, 1907
CHINA

"DON'T TELL ME WOMEN ARE NOT THE STUFF OF HEROES."
– QIU JIN

RACHEL CARSON

ENVIRONMENTALIST

Once there was a girl who loved to write stories about animals. Her name was Rachel, and she would grow up to become one of the world's most passionate guardians of the environment.

After graduating university with a degree in zoology, Rachel went back home to care for her aging mother. She found a job writing a series of radio shows about fish. No one else could make marine biology sound so exciting, and Rachel's program, called *Romance Under the Waters*, was a big hit. It showed that she was not only an amazing scientist but also a fine writer.

Despite having to earn a living and care for her mother, Rachel found time to write two beautiful books, called *The Sea Around Us* and *The Edge of the Sea*. And when her sister died, she even adopted her two nieces, raising them as her own.

Years later, Rachel and her mother moved to a little town in the country-side. There she started to notice the impact of pesticides on wildlife. At that time, farmers routinely sprayed chemicals on their crops to protect them from insects. What Rachel discovered was that these chemicals were poisoning other plants, animals, birds, and even humans. She wrote a book about it called *Silent Spring*.

The people who sold pesticides tried to stop her, but Rachel kept on talking about what she'd learned. *Silent Spring* was voted one of the most important science books ever written. It has inspired millions of people to join the environmental movement and campaign for the well-being of all species on Earth, not just our own.

MAY 27, 1907–APRIL 14, 1964
UNITED STATES OF AMERICA

ILLUSTRATION BY SARAH WILKINS

"IN NATURE
NOTHING EXISTS ALONE."
– RACHEL CARSON

RIGOBERTA MENCHÚ TUM

POLITICAL ACTIVIST

Once there was a girl who was told she didn't matter. She lived high in the mountains of Guatemala, but she and her family had to work down in the valleys picking coffee beans. The plantation owners worked them hard and beat them if they did not pick fast enough. The workers were treated like slaves and were paid hardly anything. "Your life is not worth a bag of beans," her bosses told her. "My name is Rigoberta," she replied, "and my life is worth just as much as yours."

Rigoberta was proud of her people and her culture. The Mayans of Guatemala could trace their history back to ancient times. They had a rich and wonderful civilization. But they had been forced into poverty, and they were beaten and even killed by soldiers if they dared to protest.

She started fighting for better conditions and equal rights for her people. She organized strikes and demonstrations. Although Rigoberta could not read or write, she spoke with such conviction that more and more people joined her cause. Many were taken away and killed, including Rigoberta's own parents and her brother. The government tried to silence her and the landowners tried to break her, but no one could crush her fearless spirit. She insisted on telling her story—not because it was hers but because it was the story of oppressed indigenous peoples everywhere.

Rigoberta played a large part in ending the civil war in Guatemala. For this, and for her life's work campaigning for the rights of the poor, she was awarded a Nobel Peace Prize.

BORN JANUARY 9, 1959
GUATEMALA

"I AM LIKE A DROP OF WATER ON A ROCK.
AFTER DRIP, DRIP, DRIPPING IN THE SAME PLACE,
I BEGIN TO LEAVE A MARK, AND I LEAVE MY MARK
IN MANY PEOPLE'S HEARTS."
– RIGOBERTA MENCHÚ TUM

ROSALIND FRANKLIN

· CHEMIST AND X-RAY CRYSTALLOGRAPHER

Once upon a time, there was a girl who discovered the secret of life. Her name was Rosalind, and she was an extraordinary chemist. She was also an X-ray **crystallographer** and worked as a researcher in the biophysics lab at King's College London.

Rosalind studied DNA, a molecule carrying information that tells our bodies how to develop and function. Today, we know that DNA is shaped like a double helix—basically a twisted ladder—but in Rosalind's time, the scientific community had no idea what DNA looked like.

Rosalind spent hundreds of hours using X-rays to photograph DNA fibers and trying to unveil the secret of life. She even improved the machines she used so she could get the best possible picture.

Each photo took about a hundred hours to develop. One day, her team got an incredible shot that provided groundbreaking information about the structure of DNA. They called it *Photograph 51*.

One of the scientists working with Rosalind, Maurice Wilkins, didn't like her, so without telling her, he sent the photo to two competing scientists who were also studying DNA. When those two scientists, James Watson and Francis Crick, saw the picture, their jaws dropped. They used *Photograph 51* as the basis of their 3D model of DNA, which eventually won them a Nobel Prize in Physiology or Medicine.

Rosalind left King's College London to work in other areas. She made crucial discoveries about how viruses spread infection. For this—and for her vital contribution to the discovery of DNA—she is now acknowledged as one of the most important scientists of the twentieth century.

JULY 25, 1920 - APRIL 16, 1958
UNITED KINGDOM

"SCIENCE AND EVERYDAY LIFE
CANNOT AND SHOULD NOT BE SEPARATED."
– ROSALIND FRANKLIN

RUBY NELL BRIDGES

ACTIVIST

Once upon a time in New Orleans, there lived an incredibly brave girl called Ruby. She had to walk miles to get to her school, even though there was one closer to her home. But that school was all-white, and Ruby was black. "You can't stop my child from going to a school because of the color of her skin," said Ruby's mom. "It's wrong. And it's against the law."

Even though members of the school board didn't want to admit it, they knew Ruby's mom was right. They made Ruby sit a tough exam to get in— hoping that she would fail. But Ruby wasn't just brave, she was smart too, and she aced the test.

She was excited to go to her new school, but when she and her mom arrived on her first day, they found a crowd of angry people shouting racist slogans at the gate. "I had no idea what was happening. I thought it was Mardi Gras," remembered Ruby. She was just six years old.

Each day, Ruby went to school with four United States Marshals to protect her. The sight of this small girl flanked by her big bodyguards inspired the artist Norman Rockwell to produce a famous painting called *The Problem We All Live With*.

Ruby grew up to be a brilliant civil rights activist. She even went to the White House to meet President Barack Obama, and together they looked at Rockwell's painting, which hung outside the Oval Office. "We should never look at a person and judge them by the color of their skin," Ruby said. "That's the lesson I learned in first grade."

BORN SEPTEMBER 8, 1954
UNITED STATES OF AMERICA

ILLUSTRATION BY
GIULIA TOMAI

ABCDEFGHIJKLM
NOPQRSTUVWXYZ
123456789

"DON'T FOLLOW THE PATH.
GO WHERE THERE IS NO PATH AND BEGIN THE TRAIL."
– RUBY NELL BRIDGES

SAMANTHA CRISTOFORETTI

ASTRONAUT

Once upon a time, there was an engineer who brewed coffee in outer space. Her name was Samantha, and she was also an astronaut.

Samantha had studied mechanical engineering and aeronautics at university. After she graduated, she joined a flight school and finished at the top of her class. Samantha became a fighter pilot in the Italian Air Force, but she wanted to fly even higher.

So she applied to the European Space Agency to join its space program. Only six pilots out of more than eight thousand applicants were selected: Samantha was one of them.

For two years, she went through an incredibly hard training program. At an underwater military training camp in Houston, Texas, Samantha had to learn how to assemble equipment at the bottom of a pool four times deeper than a normal one, how to swim while wearing a space suit, and how to fight under water. She even had to learn how to speak Russian!

Once she had mastered all that, she was ready to go.

At the International Space Station, Captain Cristoforetti performed over two hundred experiments to study how the human body reacts to long stretches of time spent in zero gravity. "In the future," she predicted, "the human race will live on multiple planets, so it's important to know what happens to our bodies in outer space."

During the mission, Samantha also experimented with different kinds of food. "Who would want to live on Mars," she asked, "if they could only eat stuff squeezed out of a tube?" She was the third European woman to travel to outer space—and the first person to brew coffee there!

BORN APRIL 26, 1977
ITALY

154

"ALWAYS REMEMBER, IF YOU HAVE TO CHOOSE BETWEEN AN EASY THING AND A HARD ONE, THE HARD ONE'S USUALLY A LOT MORE FUN."
— SAMANTHA CRISTOFORETTI

SAPPHO

POET

A long time ago, on a small island in the Aegean Sea called Lesbos, there lived a poet. Her name was Sappho.

Sappho had dark hair and a sweet smile. She ran a special boarding school where girls were educated in art and religion. She also wrote poems, and these were read and sung during public ceremonies, often as a farewell to the students who were ready to leave the school.

Sappho wrote about the intense emotional bond between girls and young women. In ancient Greece at that time, married women weren't able to have the close friendships they had enjoyed at school; instead, they were mostly confined to their husbands' homes. Sappho's poems celebrated the loving relationships that existed between girls, to remind older women of the friendships they had enjoyed in their younger days. The greatest writers and thinkers of the time praised her work, and she inspired many others. She even created a new form of poetry, called the **Sapphic stanza**.

She wrote her lines of verse on papyrus scrolls, some of which were carefully stored in the Great Library of Alexandria in Egypt. But over the centuries, most of the fragile scrolls were lost. Although Sappho wrote more than ten thousand lines during her life, only a few fragments of her poems have survived to the present day.

Sappho's poetry is so romantic that for thousands of years, she has symbolized women's love around the world. And that is why women who love women are called lesbians, after the beautiful Greek island where Sappho lived.

C. 610 BCE – C. 570 BCE

GREECE

ILLUSTRATION BY
ELENI KALORKOTI

"I DECLARE
THAT LATER ON,
EVEN IN AN AGE UNLIKE OUR OWN,
SOMEONE WILL REMEMBER WHO WE ARE."
– SAPPHO

SARA SEAGER

ASTROPHYSICIST

Once upon a time, there lived a girl whose mind seemed to work much faster than anyone else's. She could make connections between things in the blink of an eye. She didn't watch TV because it seemed slow and boring. She preferred to be up in her bedroom looking through her telescope.

While other people looked at the moon or the stars, Sara looked at the spaces in between. She knew that in the dark spaces, there were billions more stars, and that most of those had planets circling around them, just like the earth orbits the sun. Were they far enough from their own suns not to burn up? Were they near enough not to be permanently frozen? Were they in that sweet spot—that one chance in a million—where life could form?

Sara Seager grew up to be a real-life alien hunter. Her job at the Massachusetts Institute of Technology is to look for signs of life on exoplanets, which are planets beyond our own solar system that orbit stars in distant galaxies. In the hallway outside her office is a poster of one of them: a rocky desert with two suns burning in the sky, just like Luke Skywalker's home planet, Tatooine, in the Star Wars movies.

Sara is not very practical and admits she couldn't change a light bulb at home. But her two boys are proud of their mom—a certified genius, and one of the top astrophysicists in the world. She sometimes can't find their socks, but she might just find a whole new Earth!

BORN JULY 21, 1971
CANADA

"BEING A SCIENTIST
IS LIKE BEING
AN EXPLORER."
– SARA SEAGER

SARINYA SRISAKUL

FIREFIGHTER

One day, a young woman went to her father with some exciting news. "Dad," she said, "I've signed up to become a firefighter!" Her father was stunned. "You're crazy," he said. "It's dangerous. It's not a very good job for a woman. And anyway, we're from Thailand; there aren't any Asian people in New York's fire department." But Sarinya was determined.

She went through a tough three-month boot camp where she learned how to fight kitchen and car fires, how to maneuver aerial ladders, and how to handle lots of other challenges! She was the only woman trainee, and one of the very few who wasn't white. It was extremely hard, but she made it.

Firefighters need to be very fit to deal with all sorts of emergencies, so to keep in shape, Sarinya began to cycle from home to work and back again. Every day she faced new and unexpected situations: stuck elevators, suspicious packages, flooding, car accidents, gas leaks … "I never knew what to expect when I walked in the fire station door," Sarinya explains. "Being a firefighter is really fun and exciting, and you get to help people."

Whenever there was a woman who needed help, Sarinya was always first on the scene. "Sometimes seeing a face like your own gives a huge sense of relief to someone in an emotional state," she says. The fact that she spoke several languages was also a big advantage in New York, where there are so many people from different cultures and not everyone speaks English.

There are now twice as many women in New York's fire department as there were when she started. "That's great," says Sarinya, "but I'm still the only Asian woman firefighter. I'm really looking forward to meeting number two!"

BORN C. 1980
UNITED STATES OF AMERICA

ILLUSTRATION BY
LISK FENG

"THE MAIN THING
ABOUT BEING 'HEROIC'
IS HELPING OTHERS."
– SARINYA SRISAKUL

SELDA BAĞCAN

SINGER AND SONGWRITER

Once there was a girl who spent every night playing and singing with her brothers, pretending to be the Beatles. Her name was Selda.

When she grew up, Selda moved to the city of Ankara to study physics. Her brothers had also moved there, and they ran a popular music club called Beethoven.

Every night, Selda would put down her books, pick up her electric guitar, and head to Beethoven. The club was always packed whenever Selda played. She put a rock twist on Turkish **folk music**. Nobody had ever heard anything like it before!

Selda's music was political and her lyrics directly challenged the government. "Why is it so hard to make new roads?" she would sing. When a military regime took power in Turkey, Selda was banned from appearing on TV and arrested three times. The government even took away her passport so she couldn't leave the country.

But nobody could stop Selda's music.

Millions of people all over the world danced to her songs. When she was finally free to travel again, she headed for London, where thousands of fans were waiting for her.

Selda started touring and even set up her own record label. When she found out that two American rappers had sampled her music without her permission and without paying her, she sued their record company. She didn't win, but she wasn't mad at the artists. She said she was proud that they'd used her song to rap about the black American activist Malcolm X. "Yes, they cheated on me," she said. "But for a good cause."

BORN 1948
TURKEY

SELDA

ILLUSTRATION BY
GIULIA TOMAI

"SONGS ARE MORE DANGEROUS
THAN WEAPONS."
– SELDA BAĞCAN

SERAFINA BATTAGLIA

ANTI-MAFIA WITNESS

Serafina owned a coffee shop. Her husband was a criminal. He belonged to a violent organization called the Mafia. He and his friends would meet at her coffee shop to plot all sorts of crimes.

Serafina heard the men plotting, but she never spoke up or tried to stop them. In her twisted world, people who went to the police were despised, while those who robbed and killed were admired.

One fateful day, the men in her husband's gang turned against him. They killed him and Serafina's son. Many other women had seen their loved ones killed, but none of them had spoken out. For Serafina, though, this was too much. She realized that her silence had allowed terrible things to happen.

Wrapped in a mourning shawl, she went to court to face the men accused of killing her son. There, the most powerful Mafia bosses in Italy stood behind bars like animals in a cage. Serafina held the bars and looked the men in the eye. "You drank my son's blood," she said, "and here, before God and man, I spit in your face." And she did. Then she turned to the judge and said, "Mafia bosses have no honor."

That was the start of a ten-year collaboration between Serafina and the police. Thanks to her, officers arrested hundreds of criminals. Some of them later bribed the judges and walked free, but even so, Serafina had set an example. After her, many more women started to speak out.

"If all the women talked about what they know of their men," she said, "the Mafia would no longer exist."

1919 – SEPTEMBER 9, 2004
ITALY

164

ILLUSTRATION BY
GIORGIA MARRAS

per
Cesare
Terranova

"JUSTICE IS MY WEAPON."
– SERAFINA BATTAGLIA

SHAMSIA HASSANI

GRAFFITI ARTIST

Once upon a time, there was a girl who was an incredibly fast painter. In just a few minutes, she would create a mural and be gone. Her name was Shamsia, and she lived in Kabul, Afghanistan.

There was a good reason for Shamsia to be so quick: if she got caught making art in the streets, she would be harassed by people who believed an Afghan woman should be at home, not painting on walls. Afghanistan could be a dangerous place for women—especially those who wanted to change the rules.

Shamsia used her art to advance women's rights in her country. "Graffiti is a friendly way to fight," she said. "Most people don't go to art galleries or museums. But if I create my art in the streets, they will see it." Shamsia couldn't paint on big buildings, however, because each mural would take too much time to complete, increasing the risk of getting caught. Instead, she chose staircases, walls of narrow streets, back alleys—hidden passages that people still used on a daily basis.

She mainly painted women—big, tall women. She wanted people to notice them, and to see them in a new way. "When people see something every day—on their way to work or to school—it becomes part of their life," she explained, "and that's when they start to change their mind about something."

In one of Shamsia's murals, a girl is playing a red electric guitar. In another one, on a cracked wall near a staircase, a tall woman wearing a light blue burka is looking up toward the sky.

BORN 1988
AFGHANISTAN

ILLUSTRATION BY
CRISTINA PORTOLANO

"THE WOMEN I PAINT
ARE NOT WOMEN WHO
STAY AT HOME.
THEY ARE NEW WOMEN.
FULL OF ENERGY."
— SHAMSIA HASSANI

SIMONE VEIL

POLITICIAN

Simone could not understand war. "Why would one country want to attack another?" she asked. She was a Jewish girl living through the Second World War—one of the most violent conflicts the world had ever seen—and her whole family had been deported by the Nazis to a concentration camp.

By the time the war came to an end, Simone had lost her mom, her dad, and her brother.

She had witnessed so much injustice that she felt a great urge to do something about it. She studied law and became a judge in France.

Simone got married to a man who worked in aeronautics. One day the French president visited their home to ask her husband if he would like to join the government. By the end of the president's visit, it was Simone who was offered the job. She became the health minister in the president's cabinet.

When France and other countries decided to unite their citizens in the European Union, Simone ran to become a member of the European Parliament. She won—and even became its first president!

As president, Simone focused on reconciliation, even when that meant working with Germany, whose Nazi regime had once caused so much pain to her people. But she knew war was not—and had never been—an answer. She believed that peace and justice were worth fighting for. Simone thought that was what the European dream was about, and she devoted her life to it.

"The idea of war was for me something terrible," Simone Veil once told a journalist. "The only possible option was to make peace."

JULY 13, 1927 - JUNE 30, 2017

FRANCE

"EUROPE'S DESTINY AND
THE FUTURE OF THE
FREE WORLD ARE
ENTIRELY IN OUR HANDS."
– SIMONE VEIL

SKY BROWN

SKATEBOARDER

Once upon a time in Japan, there was a little girl called Sky. Sky's dad was a skateboarder, and she loved watching him zoom up slopes and perform amazing stunts. Although she could barely walk, Sky used to balance on his skateboard and try to copy him.

At first, Sky's dad was afraid she'd fall and hurt herself, but then he realized that she was a natural at skateboarding. He bought her a board of her very own.

When Sky went to the skate park to practice, the older boys would sometimes cut in front of her. What could this little girl know about skateboarding? Well, she knew quite a bit.

Being underestimated pushed Sky to train harder, to jump higher, and to learn more tricks. Soon, she was the youngest skater ever on the Vans Park Series, a professional skateboarding tour.

Nobody gets good at skating without suffering their share of bloody knees and scraped elbows, and Sky has tumbled off her board many times. Once, she fell in a steep bowl during a competition. She couldn't climb out on her own, but three of her fellow skaters helped her clamber to the top. They gave her a high five when she made it out.

"It's okay to fall," she thought, "when you can count on people to pick you up! I want to be just like them: a good skater and a good person."

Today, Sky continues to push the limits and challenge much older competitors in the male-dominated skateboarding world. "I prefer ramps and bowls to swings and slides—they are just sooo much more fun," she says. "Landing a flip super-clean is just so exciting. I love the feeling of it all."

BORN JULY 7, 2008
JAPAN

"WHEN I'M SCARED, I FEEL THE MOST HAPPY... AND IT'S SOOO FUN TO SEE THE LOOK ON ALL THE BOYS' FACES."
– SKY BROWN

SOFIA IONESCU

NEUROSURGEON

Once there was a girl with wonderful hands: strong and steady, with long, elegant fingers. "With hands like those, you could be a pianist or a painter," said her schoolteachers. Art and music were all very well, but Sofia had something else in mind. A young friend of hers had died following brain surgery. Sophia wanted to become a neurosurgeon to help save the lives of people like her friend.

At that time, there were hardly any female doctors in Romania, and female neurosurgeons were extremely rare everywhere in the world. Sofia's teachers didn't think she was smart enough even to get into medical school. But she studied hard, by the light of a streetlamp shining through her bedroom window, and with her mother's constant support, she passed all her courses and exams and became a doctor.

During the Second World War, Sofia volunteered to take care of wounded soldiers in the hospital near her home. She operated on them—mostly performing amputations when their arms or legs had been so badly damaged that they could not be saved. But she still wanted most of all to be a neurosurgeon, operating on the brain.

One day she got her chance. A boy was rushed into the hospital with terrible injuries to his head. None of the other surgeons were there. As bombs fell around them, Sofia took up a scalpel and looked at her hands—they were strong and steady as always. That day, she saved the young boy's life.

After the war, Sofia trained as a neurosurgeon, and through her long and distinguished career, she saved many, many more lives.

APRIL 25, 1920 – MARCH 21, 2008
ROMANIA

ILLUSTRATION BY
ELENIA BERETTA

"WHEN I PERFORMED
MY FIRST OPERATION,
NEUROSURGERY HAD JUST STARTED."
– SOFIA IONESCU

SOJOURNER TRUTH

ACTIVIST

I sabella had a powerful voice. But she couldn't use it because she was born into slavery.

When she grew up, Isabella fell in love with a man named Robert and wanted to marry him, but the family who kept him enslaved forbade him from being with her. She was forced to marry another man, Thomas, and they had five children. But Isabella never knew if she would see her children from one day to the next—the slave owners could sell them without even telling her. It was terrifying.

The man who held her captive, Dumont, promised he would set Isabella and her children free, but when the day came, he broke his word. Outraged, Isabella escaped.

Some neighbors who wanted slavery to end paid Dumont twenty dollars, and Isabella was finally set free. Now she could use her voice.

One of her sons, Peter, had been sold to a slave owner in Alabama, but Isabella knew it was illegal to sell slaves across state lines. She took the white man to court and won! Peter returned with her to New York.

Isabella changed her name to Sojourner Truth. "Sojourner" means one who travels, and she set out across the country giving speeches about the true meaning of slavery, and about the importance of equal rights for men and women.

"That man over there says that women need to be helped into carriages, and lifted over ditches," she said in one speech. "Nobody ever helps me into carriages, or over mud-puddles! And ain't I a woman?"

C. 1797-NOVEMBER 26, 1883
UNITED STATES OF AMERICA

"LOOK AT MY ARM!
AIN'T I A WOMAN?"
– SOJOURNER TRUTH

SONIA SOTOMAYOR

JUSTICE OF THE SUPREME COURT

Once there was a girl who wanted to be a detective. Her name was Sonia.

When she was six, Sonia was diagnosed with **diabetes**. "You can't be a detective," she was told. "You need to find something else!" But Sonia didn't give up. Her favorite TV show was a legal drama starring a brilliant lawyer named Perry Mason. He wasn't as exciting as her favorite detective, Nancy Drew, but he was great at solving crimes.

"Fair enough," she thought. "I'll be a lawyer like Perry Mason."

Sonia came from a poor family that had moved to New York from Puerto Rico. When she was nine, her father died, leaving her mother to provide for the entire family. She worked six days a week, and she kept telling Sonia that she had to get an excellent education.

Sonia didn't disappoint her. She studied hard and became one of the few Hispanic female students accepted by Princeton University at that time. "I felt like an alien," she later recalled. But she still managed to graduate with top grades, and she continued her studies at the prestigious Yale Law School.

She became a judge and worked at every level of the judicial system. When Barack Obama was elected president, he nominated her to the **Supreme Court** of the United States, and Sonia became the first Latina to serve in that position.

Sonia played a major role in some of the country's most important legal cases, including the historic decision to make same-sex marriage legal in all states.

BORN JUNE 25, 1954
UNITED STATES OF AMERICA

"THE LATINA IN ME IS AN EMBER
THAT BLAZES FOREVER."
– SONIA SOTOMAYOR

SOPHIA LOREN

ACTRESS

Sophia's nickname was Toothpick.

She grew up in Naples, Italy, during the Second World War, sharing a small apartment with her mom, her sister, her grandparents, and her aunt and uncle. Nobody ever had enough to eat.

Sophia's mom had often dreamt of becoming an actress, so when she heard that extras were needed on a film shoot in Rome, she packed her bags and headed off, taking Sophia with her. Sophia was still a teenager, but she realized that she liked being on set, so she decided to stay in Rome and try to become an actress herself.

By this time, the skinny little toothpick had blossomed into a beautiful young woman. Sophia worked as a model for magazines and in fashion shows while she tried to break into the movies.

Directors were attracted first by her beauty. But they quickly found out that Sophia was also an incredible actress. Soon enough, she became the face of Italian cinema. Comedies, dramas, thrillers—she starred in them all.

With her mischievous sense of humor, her passion, and her strong personality, Sophia embodied the whole country's determination to bounce back after the long, hard years of war, and to work toward a brighter future.

Hollywood also noticed Sophia's talent, and before long, producers were falling over each other to sign her to their next big film. She put that special sparkle into the golden age of American cinema.

"If you're stubborn enough," Sophia once said, "you will know which stories are closer to your heart, you will do your best to tell those stories, and eventually you'll be successful."

BORN SEPTEMBER 20, 1934
ITALY

"EVERYTHING YOU SEE
I OWE TO SPAGHETTI."
– SOPHIA LOREN

SOPHIE SCHOLL

ACTIVIST

Once upon a time, a girl named Sophie used to stand outside her town's prison walls playing her flute, hoping that one particular prisoner would hear. The tune she played was "Die Gedanken sind frei" (Your thoughts are free), and the prisoner listening in his cell was her father. He had been thrown in jail because he was opposed to the Nazis and their leader, Adolf Hitler.

When she was younger, Sophie had supported Hitler. She and her brother Hans had even marched in parades for him. But then they started reading about the terrible things the Nazis were doing. They learned about the mass murder of Jews and other unwanted people, and they realized their father had been right from the start: Adolf Hitler was not a good man.

Sophie and Hans formed a group called the White Rose and produced flyers and pamphlets encouraging Germans to resist the Nazis.

At that time, every school, church, university, and street was full of spies, and anyone who dared criticize Hitler was reported to the police and arrested. But that didn't stop Sophie. She knew in her heart that opposing the Nazi Party was the right thing to do, and she wasn't afraid of the consequences.

"How can we expect justice to prevail if we don't give ourselves up for a just cause?" she said.

Sadly, Sophie and the other members of the White Rose were arrested, tried, and executed by the Nazis, but their example inspired people all over the world to fight for freedom.

MAY 9, 1921–FEBRUARY 22, 1943
GERMANY

"WHAT DOES MY DEATH MATTER
IF, THROUGH US, THOUSANDS
OF PEOPLE ARE STIRRED
TO ACTION?"
– SOPHIE SCHOLL

STEFFI GRAF

TENNIS PLAYER

Once there was a little girl who loved tennis. Steffi would watch her father coaching all the other players and follow him around, pestering him to let her play too.

"Papa, I want a racket. I want to play tennis like you."

"You're too small," her father would say. "Wait until you have grown up a little more."

"But I want to play now!"

She bugged him so much that finally he gave in. He picked up a tennis racket and chopped the handle in half.

"There," he said. "Now you can play."

Steffi was thrilled. She made her own little tennis court in the basement, tying a piece of string between two chairs for the net. She spent hours downstairs, blissfully banging the ball with her racket. She was very happy. Her mother was not so happy, though—a lot of lamps got broken!

When she was just six years old, Steffi won her first tennis tournament, and from then on, there was no stopping her. She grew up to be one of the most brilliant tennis stars in the world. She won twenty-two Grand Slam singles titles, captured an Olympic gold medal, and was voted German sports personality of the year a record-breaking five times!

Now she loves spending time with her daughter, Jaz, who prefers roller-skating and hip-hop dance to tennis. Steffi doesn't mind. She believes that every little girl should be free to do what she loves and what makes her happy.

BORN JUNE 14, 1969
GERMANY

"I STARTED MY CAREER IN MY LIVING ROOM.
MY DAD THREW THE BALL AND I HIT IT—I DESTROYED
A LOT OF FURNITURE."
— STEFFI GRAF

TEMPLE GRANDIN

PROFESSOR OF ANIMAL SCIENCES

Once upon a time, there was a girl who invented a hug machine. Her name was Temple, and she didn't speak until she was three and a half years old. Luckily, her parents realized she needed a little extra help and hired a speech therapist for her.

Temple's mom could see that her daughter was different, but she didn't realize until later that she was autistic. An autistic person's brain is wired slightly differently, and her experience of the world is different from other people's as a result. Like many autistic children, Temple had super-sensitive skin: she found clothes really itchy, so she always had to wear very soft pants and shirts. She also didn't like to be hugged, but she loved the feeling of being pressed, so she invented a machine that could hug her just the way she wanted.

At that time, people didn't understand autism. They didn't want to be labeled as autistic, even though that can mean many different things. Autistic children are on a spectrum that can range from genius level to a child with severe developmental disabilities or no language at all. But Temple was not afraid to speak about her autism, and to explain the different way her brain worked. "I don't think in words," she liked to say. "I think in pictures, just like a cow!"

Temple instinctively understood how animals make sense of the world. She became a world-famous professor of animal sciences and argued strongly for the humane treatment of livestock in a brilliant book called *Animals Make Us Human*.

BORN AUGUST 29, 1947
UNITED STATES OF AMERICA

"THE MOST IMPORTANT THING PEOPLE DID FOR ME
WAS TO EXPOSE ME TO NEW THINGS."
– TEMPLE GRANDIN

TROOP 6000

GIRL SCOUTS

Giselle was a single mother with five children.

She worked hard to pay the rent on their low-cost apartment. But when the landlord sold the building, she couldn't afford another place, and she and her kids found themselves homeless.

The city of New York had rented ten floors to shelter homeless families at a motel in the Queens neighborhood, and that's where Giselle and her children went.

At the time, Giselle was working at the Girl Scouts of Greater New York, so she thought, "Why not start a troop in the shelter?" And she did.

At the first meeting, there were only eight girls, and three of them were Giselle's own daughters. But she didn't give up. Through word of mouth and flyers, Troop 6000 grew to twenty-eight members, some as young as five years old.

"Being homeless is not easy," Giselle said. "I hope the girls in Troop 6000 learn that tough times are just seasons in their lives. And that they will surpass it."

Troop 6000 is the first one for homeless girls in New York City, but many more will follow—unfortunately, homelessness is still a serious problem across America. "We are like a pack," said Giselle's daughter Karina. "If one of us is down, the rest of us will be there to pick them back up."

Like other Girl Scouts and Girl Guides, Karina and her friends love adventure. They cultivate courage and honesty, responsibility and strength. They know that no matter where you're from or where you live, that's what being a Girl Scout is all about!

STARTED FEBRUARY 2017
UNITED STATES OF AMERICA

ILLUSTRATION BY
ALICE BARBERINI

"THERE IS SO MUCH MORE OUT THERE
THAT YOU'RE CAPABLE OF ACCOMPLISHING!"
– GISELLE BURGESS

VALENTINA TERESHKOVA

COSMONAUT

Once upon a time, there was an eighty-year-old woman who wanted to volunteer for a one-way trip to Mars. Her name was Valentina, and back when she was twenty-four, she was the first woman to travel to outer space.

Valentina loved to fly. She would parachute every weekend, during the day or at night, onto land and into water. When Russia started selecting women to train as cosmonauts, Valentina did her best to get into the program. After months of hard training, she was chosen to fly aboard the spacecraft *Vostok 6*.

Soon after takeoff, though, Valentina realized that something was wrong. The settings for reentry were incorrect, and at the end of the mission, they would have sent the craft shooting off into outer space instead of back to Earth. As much as she loved flying, Valentina wasn't ready to leave Earth for good just yet! So she got in touch with the engineers back at mission control, and everyone worked frantically to correct the settings before it was too late.

Her bosses were horrified and didn't want to admit they'd made a mistake. They made Valentina promise she'd never tell anyone. Thirty years passed before she could reveal the truth about her mission.

Now that she's an old woman, Valentina would love to blast off into space on one final voyage. "The earth looks so beautiful and fragile from outer space," she says. "We must do our best to protect it. Especially from asteroids."

BORN MARCH 6, 1937
RUSSIA

ILLUSTRATION BY
MALIN ROSENQVIST

"HEY, SKY, TAKE OFF YOUR HAT. I'M ON MY WAY!"
— VALENTINA TERESHKOVA

CCCP

VALERIE THOMAS

ASTRONOMER

One day, a young girl picked up a book called *The Boys' First Book of Radio and Electronics*. "I'm not a boy," thought Valerie. "But who cares? This is really fascinating!"

When her dad took apart their television to fix it, Valerie wanted to help. "This is too complicated for girls," her father said, but she wanted to find out how things worked.

After university, she got a top job at NASA working on something way more complicated than a television: the world's first satellite. *Landsat 1* was launched into space, and it sent back images of the earth that helped predict weather patterns and crop cycles.

Then one day, Valerie visited a science museum and saw something that would change her life. It was a light bulb, sitting on its own, with no connections, and shining brightly! How did they do that?

The answer was a clever optical illusion created by a hidden second light bulb and **concave mirrors** that made it *look* as if the first bulb was on. That gave Valerie a great idea. She began to research concave mirrors and light at NASA, and she came up with a brilliant invention called the **illusion transmitter**. This amazing piece of technology is still used in NASA's space exploration programs, and scientists like Valerie are developing ways to use it to look inside the human body. One day, it may also project 3D videos from your television right into your living room!

"Figure out what you want, fight the power, live without limits," Valerie says. "You won't figure it out if you just play by the rules and listen obediently."

BORN MAY 1943
UNITED STATES OF AMERICA

"FIGURING OUT WHAT YOU WANT
COMES FROM FAILING, AND THEN
TRYING AGAIN."
– VALERIE THOMAS

VIOLETA PARRA

COMPOSER AND MUSICIAN

Once upon a time, there was a girl who used to sing with her sister while cleaning gravestones at the cemetery. Her name was Violeta.

Violeta didn't have beautiful dresses to wear. Her family was poor, so her mother made her dresses from scraps of material. Violeta didn't mind. In fact, she thought her clothes were so beautiful that even when she was grown up and had money of her own, she decided to keep dressing that way.

One day, she and her sister passed a farm and heard some workers singing a beautiful song. "I love that song so much!" Violeta exclaimed. So when she got home, she found her father's guitar and began to play. Her fingers danced across the strings, making the most enchanting music.

When she got older, Violeta started to travel across Chile. With a recorder and notebook in hand, she went to the remotest corners of the country, gathering songs and memories from all the people she met. Many of the songs she learned had been passed from generation to generation, but no one had ever written them down or recorded them before Violeta came along.

Her music was deeply inspired by the traditional folk culture she had absorbed during her journey. Violeta became a national hero. Her songs spoke of legends, history, love, and life.

Violeta was also a sculptor, a poet, and a painter. And she embroidered pictures that were so beautiful, they were exhibited at the Louvre Museum in Paris after her death.

Today, Violeta's songs are sung all over the world.

OCTOBER 4, 1917 – FEBRUARY 5, 1967

CHILE

ILLUSTRATION BY
PAOLA ROLLO

"DON'T CRY WHEN THE SUN IS
GONE, BECAUSE THE TEARS
WON'T LET YOU SEE THE STARS."
– VIOLETA PARRA

VIRGINIA HALL

SPY

Once upon a time, there was a woman with a wooden leg. Her name was Virginia, and she called her leg Cuthbert.

Though she walked with a limp, Virginia was amazingly determined. When the Second World War broke out, she joined the British Special Forces and set off across the English Channel to help the French Resistance fight the Nazis.

Virginia was a master of disguise. One time, she pretended to be an elderly milkmaid. She dyed her hair gray, put on a long skirt, and shuffled along so no one could see she had a limp. She managed to send out secret radio messages telling the Allies about German troop movements. It was incredibly dangerous, and Virginia knew that if she were discovered she would be tortured and killed. But she carried on regardless.

The Limping Lady, as she was known, was considered the most dangerous of all Allied spies. The Nazi secret police put up wanted posters all over France, but Virginia always stayed one step ahead of them.

Once, she almost died crossing the Pyrenees Mountains on foot in the middle of winter. She radioed a message to London: "Having trouble with Cuthbert." They didn't realize she was talking about her leg. "If Cuthbert is giving you difficulty," they replied, "have him eliminated!"

By the end of the war, the Limping Lady's team had destroyed four bridges, derailed several freight trains, blown up a railway line, cut down telephone wires, and captured hundreds of enemy soldiers. Virginia was declared America's greatest female spy and received a medal for her bravery.

APRIL 6, 1906 – JULY 8, 1982
UNITED STATES OF AMERICA

"AFTER ALL, MY NECK
IS MY OWN. IF I AM
WILLING TO GET A
CRICK IN IT, I THINK
THAT'S MY CHOICE."
- VIRGINIA HALL

VIVIAN MAIER

PHOTOGRAPHER

Once there was a nanny who was a secret photographer. She would walk the streets of Chicago with the children she was looking after and photograph strangers going about their daily lives. Her name was Vivian. She never showed her pictures to anyone.

Vivian lived for forty years with the families she worked for. She didn't like to talk and asked for locks for her room, which she forbade anyone to enter. She was so secretive that when she took her film rolls to be developed, she never gave her real name. Over the course of her life, she took more than a hundred thousand pictures, but nobody ever knew she was a photographer.

Vivian kept all her negatives and prints in a rented storage space. Two years before she died, she failed to pay the rent, and everything inside was put up for sale. At the auction, all of her work was bought by three photo collectors. They had no idea they had found a treasure trove.

Despite having no formal training, Vivian had captured the street life of postwar America with the rawness and intensity of a master—people eating doughnuts, shopping for groceries, going to museums, being arrested, kissing, selling newspapers, cleaning shoes. Sometimes she also took pictures of herself—as seen in the reflection of shop windows, or even as a shadow on a wall.

She became a worldwide sensation.

She used a Rolleiflex camera, held at chest level so she could maintain eye contact with the person she was photographing. Many of her most memorable shots are of people staring straight at her.

FEBRUARY 1, 1926 – APRIL 21, 2009
UNITED STATES OF AMERICA

"I'M SORT OF A SPY."
— VIVIAN MAIER

WISŁAWA SZYMBORSKA

POET

Once, many years ago, a little girl handed a piece of paper to her father. On it was a poem she had written. Her father put on his glasses and studied the wobbly handwriting very seriously. Then he nodded, reached into his pocket, and pulled out a penny. "It is a good poem, Wisława," he said, giving the coin to his daughter with a smile.

Wisława's house was full of books. She read everything she could and wrote poetry throughout her childhood. Although her family wasn't rich, it was a happy house, full of chatter and laughter and books and cats.

Everything changed when the Second World War broke out. Led by Hitler, the German army invaded Wisława's homeland of Poland when she was sixteen. It was a terrible time for Jewish people like her. She still wrote poetry, but it had to be in secret. If the Nazis had found her poems—especially one that poked fun at Hitler as a baby, calling him "a little fellow in his itty-bitty robe"—she would have been killed.

Over the course of the war, millions of European Jews were taken to concentration camps and murdered, but Wisława miraculously managed to survive—and to keep writing. People everywhere loved her poetry because she wrote simply and beautifully about all sorts of ordinary things: "chairs and sorrows, scissors, tenderness, transistors, violins, [and] tea-cups." She also found fun and laughter in unexpected places. When she won a Nobel Prize in Literature, she joked that it was all because her friend had a "magic sofa." If you sat in it, you would get the prize!

JULY 2, 1923 – FEBRUARY 1, 2012
POLAND

ILLUSTRATION BY
ZOSIA DZIERŻAWSKA

"IN EVERY
POSSIBLE ANSWER,
THERE SHOULD BE
ANOTHER
QUESTION."
– WISŁAWA SZYMBORSKA

YEONMI PARK

ACTIVIST

Once upon a time, in North Korea, people were not free to sing, to wear what they wanted, to read a newspaper, or to make a phone call abroad.

Yeonmi was born there. Like many North Koreans, she was so scared of the supreme leader that she thought he could read her mind and would imprison her if he didn't like her thoughts.

When Yeonmi was fourteen, her family decided to escape.

It was a dangerous journey. She and her mother crossed a frozen river and three mountains to get to the Chinese border. There, they were treated very badly. When refugees have no option but to enter a country illegally, they have no laws to protect them and can fall victim to all sorts of criminals.

Yeonmi and her mother lived in hiding, terrified that the Chinese authorities would find them and send them back to North Korea. It was so scary that they fled again to Mongolia.

They walked across the Gobi Desert using a compass. When it stopped working, they followed the stars. At the Mongolian border, the guards told them they couldn't cross. Having lost all hope, Yeonmi and her mother threatened to kill themselves. The guards let them pass.

A few years later, Yeonmi, now living safely in New York City, told her story in a powerful speech at the One Young World Summit in Ireland. Her words moved the world and she became a full-time activist for human rights. Every day, she works to liberate her birth country from its terrible dictatorship and to protect North Korean refugees.

BORN OCTOBER 4, 1993
NORTH KOREA

CHINA

NORTH
KOREA

YELLOW
SEA

SOUTH
KOREA

1984

GEORGE
ORWELL

"I FELT
ONLY THE
STARS WERE
WITH US."
– YEONMI PARK

WRITE YOUR STORY

Once upon a time, _____

_____

_____

_____

_____

_____

_____

_____

_____

_____

_____

_____

_____

_____

_____

_____

_____

_____

_____

_____

_____

_____

DRAW YOUR PORTRAIT

GLOSSARY

BOYCOTT To choose not to buy something or not to participate in an event as a form of protest.

CALICO CLOTH A fabric made of heavy cotton.

CONCAVE MIRROR

A mirror with the reflecting surface curved inward.

CRYSTALLOGRAPHER

A scientist who studies how atoms are arranged in crystalline solids such as table salt, diamonds, or snowflakes.

DIABETES A disease that affects how the body processes glucose.

DOWN SYNDROME A condition caused by an extra chromosome. People with Down syndrome may have health problems, learning impairments, and physical limitations.

ENIGMATIC Said of something that is mysterious or difficult to understand.

ENZYMES Substances that speed up biochemical reactions in plants or animals.

FLORA AND FAUNA

All the plant life (flora) and animal life (fauna) present in a particular region.

FOLK MUSIC Traditional music originating with the ordinary people of a country or an area and usually transmitted orally from generation to generation.

FOOT-BINDING An ancient Chinese tradition that required little girls to have their feet broken and tightly bound, in order to change their shape and keep them impossibly small. Girls with bound feet could barely walk on their own, but their small feet were considered a sign of beauty.

GLOSSARY

GLUCOSE The main type of sugar in the blood, and the main source of energy for the body's cells.

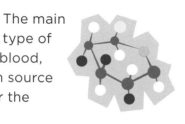

ILLUSION TRANSMITTER

A device that uses concave mirrors to create the illusion of a 3D object.

QUANTUM THEORY Classical physics describes the behavior of matter and energy in the everyday universe. It explains, for example, the motion of a baseball flying through the air. Quantum theory, on the other hand, describes the behavior of the universe on a much smaller scale. The smallest particles of the universe don't behave according to the same principles as big objects. They have their own rules, and those rules are what quantum mechanics studies.

RWANDAN GENOCIDE The mass killing of a people called the Tutsi by members of another group called the Hutu in the East African country of Rwanda in 1994.

SALSA A type of Latin American dance music, or a popular form of dance performed to this music.

SANTERÍA A religion originally practiced in Cuba but developed by people of West African descent.

SAPPHIC STANZA A group of verses of four lines, each with a specific pattern of accents and number of syllables.

SUPERSONIC PRESSURE TUNNEL

An enormous wind tunnel where NASA scientists tested space vehicles before launching them into orbit.

SUPREME COURT The highest court in the United States. It hears cases on criminal and constitutional matters.

ZERO-POINT ENERGY The lowest possible energy that a quantum mechanical system may have.

REBELS' HALL OF FAME

Let's hear it for the rebel girls and boys who were early believers in *Good Night Stories for Rebel Girls 2* on Kickstarter! They come from all over the world and they are going to change the world.

ABBIGAIL SKETCHLEY
ABBY AND PAIGE LAROCHELLE
ABIG SUSSMAN
ABIGAIL COHEN
ABIGAIL AND MADELINE SHERLOCK
ADA TAFLINGER-AHMAD
ADA WHITMAN
ADDISON AND ANDREA KANNAS
ADDISON MOYER
ADELINE HOLMSTROM
ADELKA VYCHODILOVA
ADILYNN CROCKER
AINSLEY BRIGHT
ALAINA BOWMAN
ALANA MARTINEZ HERNANDEZ
ALBA MOORE
ALDEN ECKMAN
ALEX SKALETSKY
ALEX WATKINS
ALEXA CONNELLY
ALEXANDRA FRANCES RENNIE
ALEXANDRA LISTER
ALICE BRYANT
ALICE VINCENT
ALINA GRICE
ALINA SUESS
ALISON GARCIA
ALISZA DEVIR
ALLISON COOPER
ALMA MY AND MARIE ELISE AGERLUND KAABER
ALMA OPHELIA AND HARLOW MAGDALENA ZELLERS
AMELIA AND KRISTINA CLARK
AMELIA LOOKHART
AMELIA JANE AND LOLA ELIZABETH STINSON
AMELIE BLECHNER
AMÉLIE WILLIAMS
ANA MARTIN
ANARCELIA CHAVEZ
ANGELISE KIARA RODRIGUEZ

ANIKA AND CLAUDIA STADTMUELLER
ANISHA NAYYAR
ANITA AND ANGELINA BAGGIO BARRETO
ANNA GRAFFAGNINO
ANNABEL ROSE MURPHY
ANNE DARWIN BROOKS
ANNIKA KAPLAN BASDEVANT
ANONYMOUS REBEL MOM
ANOUK AND FELIX FREUDENBERG
ANOUSHKA AND OSKAR ROBB
ANUSHRI KAHN
ARWEN AND HANNAH GREENOUGH
ARYANNA HOYEM
ASHLEY AND SHAVEA SCHLOSS
ATHENA FLEARY
AUDREY GIUSTOZZI
AVA AND KEIRA KLISS
AVA EMILY AND NOA STARLIGHT MESLER
AVA TSIGOUNIS
AVELYN CLARE CUTLER
AVERIE ANNE EVINS
AVERY AND MILA DOROGI
AVERY KEPLINGER
AYAKO ROSE SAFRENO
AYLA AND ASHLEA GRIGG
AZUL ZAPATA-TORRENEGRA
BABOOMBA TERRY
BELLA AND GIA DI MARTINO
BELLA AND GABI RIDENHOUR
BIANCA AND FEDERICO BARATTA
BILLIE KARLSSON
BRESYLN, ARROT, AND BRAXON PLESH
   STOCK-BRATINA
BRIANA FEUERSTEIN
BROOKLYN CRISOSTOMO
CAITLIN ELIZABETH DRAGONSLAYER
CAITLIN AND IMOGEN O'BRIEN
CAMILA ARNOLD
CAMILLE HANLEY

CARA QUINN LARKIN
CAROLINE ROCCASALVA
CAROLINE ROMPEL
CAROLINE SMYTH
CASSIA GLADYS CADAN-PEMAN
CATHERINE AND BECCA VAN LENT
CHANDLER GRACE OCTETREE
CHARLEE VINCELETTE
CHARLIE GRACE EVANS
CHARLIE TRUSKOSKI
CHARLOTTE AND EISLEY CLINE
CHARLOTTE KENNEDY
CHARLOTTE MOSER-JONES
CHARLOTTE POOLOS
CHIHARU BRIDGEWATER
CHLOE ANGYAL
CHLOE AND GRACE HALE
CHLOE HOBBS
CLAIRE BUSENBARK
CLAIRE DAVIS
CLAIRE POGGIE
CLAIRE RUFFY
CLAIRE AND SLOANE STOLEE
CLARA BOTELHO HOFFMANN
CLARA TOULMIN
CLEMENTINE TAFLINGER
COCO CANTRELL
COLETTE AND ASTRID UNGARETTI
CONSTANÇA VIEIRA
CORA AND IVY BRAND
DAKOTA ALLARD
DANIELA MENDEZ CASTRO
DAPHNE MARIE BARRAILLER
DASCHA MAKORI
DEBRA LOUISE AND MILLIE RUSSELL MCLEOD
DEEDEE AND NAIMA REISS-REINITZ
DELANEY KUHN
DELANEY MCSHANE
DELANEY O'CONNER
DIYA AND ISHA THOBHANI
DYLAN COOPER
EADIE MCMAHON
ELAINA MAE SCOTT
ELENA HOROBIN-HULL
ELENA WOLFE
ELIANA AND ARABELLA ARCHUNDE
ELISE LEHRKAMP
ELIZABETH "BETSY" NAGLE
ELIZABETH WEBSTER-MCFADDEN
ELLA MAGUIRE
ELLA AND AUDREY THOMPSON

ELLIA AND VICTORIA WHITACRE
ELLIE DIEBLING
ELLIE HUGHES
ELLISON AMERICA MARUSIC-REID
ELSA PORRATA
EMERI PEERY
EMERY MATTHEW
EMIE WATSON
EMILIA LEVINSEN
EMILY ALESSANDRA AND ANDREA JULIANNA
    DIFEDERICO
EMILY FENSTER
EMILY SMITH
EMMA AND LILIANNE BRUNNER
EMMA AND CHARLOTTE DAVISON
EMMA DEEG
EMMA GOMEZ
EMMA AND LUCY GROSS
EMMA HERON
EMMA ROSE MORRIS
EMMALINE JOANNE SINCLAIR
ENARA BECK
EVE NUNNIKHOVEN
EVELYN AND LYDIA HARE
EVIE GRACE CUNNINGHAM
EVIE AND JESSICA HIGGINSON
FIONA CARIELLO
FLORENCE GRACE AND AUDREY ROSE ARCHER
FRANCESCA PORRAS
FREDRICA THODE
FREJA AND JULIANA HOFVENSCHIOELD
FREYA BERGHAN-WHYMAN
GABBY AND ALEX SPLENDORIO
GABRIELA CUNHA
GABRIELLA AND GALEN VERBEELEN
GEMMA AND DARA WOMACK
GIULIA AND GIORGIA PERSICO
GRACE MARIE ASHMORE
GRACE AND SOFIA MCCOLLUM
GRACIE FOWLER
GRETA AND LUCY HUBER
GRETCHEN PELLE
HADLEY WELLS
HALLIE JO VAUGHN
HANA AND SAMANTHA HALE
HANA HEGAZY
HANNA HART
HANNAH HUNDERMARK
HANSON CCC
HARRIET STUART
HAZEL MAE CARDENAS

HELEN CLARK
HELENA AND NANCY MARTINEZ
HELENA VAN DER MERWE
HENRY TIGER AND BILLY JAMES BEVIS
TEAM HOWARD
ILAINA AND ELIAS NEWBERRY
ILORA AND VIVIKA PAL
IMOGEN OAKENFOLD
INGRID PALACIOS
IONA MARQUIST
ISABELLA ROSE FARRELL-JACKSON
ISABELLA SINENI
ISLA IYER
JACK WILLIAM AND BILLIE ROSE OLIVER
JADE REISTERER
JAHNAVI KAKARALA
JANE AND NORA ANNA BEGLEY
JASMINE GOODSON
JAZMIN ELENES-LEON
JENIFER AND ELIZABETH PATTERSON
JENNA BERARIU
JENNIFER MCCANN
JILLIAN JOY WELLS
JODI HOLLAND
JOHANA "JO-JO" HAARMAN-FOWLER
JOSEPHINE AND LUCIA MOXEY
JOSEPHINE WEBSTER-FOX
JOSIE HOPKINS
JOSIE AND NORA HUTTON
JOY AND GRACE BRADBURY-SMITH
JULIA AND PAULINA KIRSTEN
JUNIPER RUTH MARKS
JUPITER ROSE JAY
KAHUTAIKI AND AWATEA CALMAN
KAIA MARIE PADILLA
KATE TYLER
KATERYNA ZIKOU
KATHLEEN AND DAISY KELLY
KATIE MCDOWELL
KATIE MCNAB
KATIE AND LIZZIE STANDEN
KAYA GASTELUM
KAYLAH PAYNE
KELLY ROTH
KEPLER VAN OVERLOOP
KIERA JOHNSON
DR. KRISTEN LEE
KRYSTIN AND ELISSA SCHLEH
KYLA PATEL
KYLEE CAUSER
KYLIE AND KAITLYN SCOTT

KYRA MAI
LANA VERONITA DAHL
LARA IDA AND DERYA KINAY
LAUREN KROFT
LEELA AIYAGARI
LENNON AND ARIA BACKO
LEO LALONDE
LEONIE POMPEI
LILA YINGLING
LILIANA GAIA POPESCU
LILITH AND ROSE WATTERS
LILLY HAWES
LILY SCHMITT
LOLA VEGA
LUCILE ORR
LUIZA AND EMILIJA VIKTORIA GIRNIUS
LUNA PUCKETT
MACY JANE HEWS
MACY AND KATE SCHULTE
MADELEINE DALE
MADELINE GIBBS
MADELINE ANNE TERESA HAZEL-GOLDHAMER AND
    SARA NEIL LEA HAZEL
MADELINE PITTS
MADELINE AND ELAINE WOO
MADELYN O'BRIEN
MADISON ROSE HORGAN
MADISYN, MALLORY, AND RAPHAEL PLUNKETT
MAE AND EVE BUTLER
MAE BETTY AND MARGOT ROATH
MAGGIE CRISP OXFORD
MAHREYA AND CHRYSEIS GREEN
MAISIE MAZOKI
MAPLE SAN
MARGARET QUINN
MARGAUX BEDIEE
MARIELLA SCHWIETER
MARLOE MARIE NELSON
MATHILDE AND LINDA GIO COIS
MATILDA WINEBRENNER
MAYA AND NOA GUIZZI
MAYA AND SONIA TOLIA
MIA AND JADE GAVONI
MIA MICHUDA
MIA VENTURATO
MILA KONAR
MILLIE AND SLOANE KAULENTIS
MIRABELLE CHOE
MISCHA BAHAT
MOLLY DEANE
MOXIE INES GOTTLIEB

MOXIE MARQUIS
NADIA GARBE
NATALIA MACIAS PEREZ
NATALIA AND GABRIELA SHANER LOPEZ
NATALIE HEPBURN
NAYARA VIEIRA
NIAMH CAVOSKI MURPHY
NINA JOANNA ARYA
NINA HEWRYK
NORA BAILEY-RADFORD
NORA BELCHER
NORA IGLESIAS POZA
NORAH WALSH
NORENE COSTA
NORI ELIZABETH COOPER
OLIVE SARAH AND EDIE QUINN COLLINGWOOD
OLIVE SHEEHAN
OLIVIA AND MILA CAPPELLO
OLIVIA ANNA CAVALLO STEELE
OLIVIA AND AMELIA O'CONNELL
OLIVIA REED
OLIVIA YIATRAS
PEARL FUHRMAN
PENELOPE SCHNEIDER RIEHLE
PENELOPE JOY ARGUILLA TULL
PENELOPE WHITE
PEYTON AND CAMBRIA HINCY
PHOEBE BISHOP
PIPPA LUNA BARTON
PIXI JUDE RUDY
QUINN SCHULTE
REBECCA WHITE
RILEY KNEZ
RILEY AND GABRIELA ROSARIO
ROBIN AND ANNALISE NORDSTROM
ROSA AND AUSTIN KEREZSI
ROSE GOUGH
ROSE LANDRUM
ROSE LEIGHTON
ROSE TYLER
ROWAN WEBER
ROXY LEVEY
RUBY JANE MCGOWAN
RUTH BROWN
RUTHIE GEISDORFER
RYAN ACKERMAN
RYAN AND SHANE COMSTOCK FERRIS
SAOIRSE AND FELICIA BEDRIN
SARA SAEZ
SHAI MANDELL
SIENNA AND ALEXA MARTINEZ CORZINE

SIRI DIRIX
SLOANE ZELLER
SOFÍA RUÍZ-MURPHY
SOFIE PETRU
SONIA AND BEN TWEITO
SONORA SOFIA GOEL
SOPHIA AND MAYA CRISTOFORETTI
SOPHIA MARTIN
SOPHIA VUU
SOPHIE WEBB
SORAYA ALIABADI
STEIN FT
STELLA ANDERSON
STELLA MESSINA
SYDNEY BROOK
SYDNEY KERPELMAN
SYDNEY MESSER
SYLVIE FRY
SYNIA CASPER
TARA AND TALIA DAIL
TARA LEIJEN
TATE HINERFELD
TATE PITCHER
TATUM STEVELEY
TEAGAN HALEY
TEAGEN AND ANNEN GOUDELOCK
TEDDY ROSE WYLDER HEADEY
VALENTINA NUILA
VANESSA EMSLEY
VANJA SCHUBERT
VICTOR CASAS
VICTORIA AND EMMA HEDGES
VICTORIA PAYTON WOLF
VIOLET SUDBURY
VIVIAN HARRIS
VIVIAN LEE WARTHER
VIVIANA GUTIERREZ
WALLIS STUNTZ
WEDNESDAY FIONA WHITE
WILEMS GIRLS
WYNN GAUDET
ZELDA NATIV
ZOE AND SELLA ALPERIN
ZOE MAE JACKSON
ZOE AND CAILEY MCKITTRICK
ZOIE JONAKIN
ZOYA ESFAHANI

ILLUSTRATORS

Fifty extraordinary female artists from all over the world portrayed the pioneers in *Good Night Stories for Rebel Girls 2*. Here are their names!

T.S. ABE **USA**, 41, 137
CRISTINA AMODEO **ITALY**, 47, 73, 133, 175
ALICE BARBERINI **ITALY**, 49, 89, 187
ALICE BENIERO **ITALY**, 27, 113
ELENIA BERETTA **ITALY**, 11, 173
MARIJKE BUURLAGE **NETHERLANDS**, 79
CLAUDIA CARIERI **ITALY**, 51, 55, 63
BEATRICE CEROCCHI **ITALY**, 185
BARBARA DZIADOSZ **GERMANY**, 21, 105
ZOSIA DZIERŻAWSKA **POLAND**, 9, 199
JOANA ESTRELA **PORTUGAL**, 159, 201
MARYLOU FAURE **UK**, 31, 77
LISK FENG **CHINA**, 99, 161
GIULIA FLAMINI **ITALY**, 181
MONICA GARWOOD **USA**, 29, 121
DEBORA GUIDI **ITALY**, 87, 149
KATHRIN HONESTA **INDONESIA**, 177
ANA JUAN **SPAIN**, 33, 37, 61
LAURA JUNGER **FRANCE**, 101
ELENI KALORKOTI **UK**, 43, 135, 157
PRIYA KURIYAN **INDIA**, 143
LIEKELAND **NETHERLANDS**, 151, 169
GIORGIA MARRAS **ITALY**, 15, 119, 145, 165
SARAH MAZZETTI **ITALY**, 13, 71, 139
MARINA MUUN **AUSTRIA**, 125

SALLY NIXON **USA**, 5
SARA OLMOS **SPAIN**, 127, 197
MARTINA PAUKOVA **SLOVAKIA**, 7, 85
LAURA PÉREZ **SPAIN**, 65
CAMILLA PERKINS **USA**, 95, 191
CRISTINA PORTOLANO **ITALY**, 19, 83, 167, 181
KATE PRIOR **USA**, 141, 171
PAOLA ROLLO **ITALY**, 75, 193
MALIN ROSENQVIST **SWEDEN**, 67, 189
DALILA ROVAZZANI **ITALY**, 195
JÚLIA SARDÀ **SPAIN**, 111
MARTA SIGNORI **ITALY**, 17, 69, 179
NOA SNIR **ISRAEL**, 57, 93
CRISTINA SPANÒ **ITALY**, 35, 45
GAIA STELLA **ITALY**, 59
LIZZY STEWART **UK**, 53, 107
ELISABETTA STOINICH **ITALY**, 117, 123
GERALDINE SY **PHILIPPINES**, 81
GIULIA TOMAI **ITALY**, 3, 153, 155, 163
THANDIWE TSHABALALA **SOUTH AFRICA**, 91
ELINE VAN DAM **NETHERLANDS**, 23, 103, 129
ANNALISA VENTURA **ITALY**, 109, 115
EMMANUELLE WALKER **CANADA**, 25
SARAH WILKINS **NEW ZEALAND**, 97, 147
PING ZHU **USA**, 39, 131

ACKNOWLEDGMENTS

Our biggest, most heartfelt, loudest thank-you goes to our rebel community on Kickstarter. All of you—once again—responded with such generosity and enthusiasm to *Good Night Stories for Rebel Girls 2*. Not only did you back the campaign, but you helped us find these incredible stories, you cheered for us along the way, and above all, you kept believing in us.

A special thank-you also goes to all the rebel boys and men who are reading these stories and are brave enough to fight this battle alongside the women in their life.

Thank you, dads who are raising free, independent, strong daughters.

To our own dads, Angelo and Uccio, thank you for always supporting us. Even when we challenged you, even when you didn't understand our choices, you were *always* on our side. Thank you for instilling in us a burning desire for discovery and adventure, and a deep love for the places we come from.

Thank you, thank you, thank you, rebel team: Patricia, Shantèe, Breana, Emilio, Maria, John, McCall, Michon, Michael, Marisela, Eleonora. It is an honor to work with you every day.

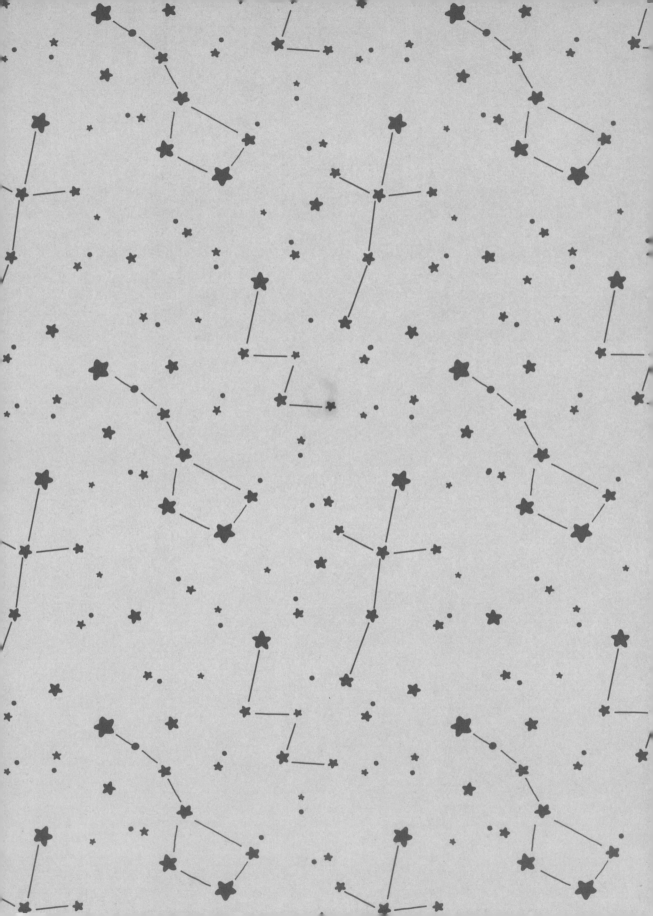